Box That Bitch

Silence Your Inner Jerk and Make Your Mind
Work for You Instead of Against You

Misty Weltzien
CLU®, ChFC®, CFP®

Copyright © 2020 by Misty Weltzien. All rights reserved.

ISBN: 9798556611672

Acknowledgments

When you write a book, they tell you to keep the acknowledgments list short. There are too many people I want to thank for their contributions to my life, so please just skip these pages if you don't want to read them!

To my parents: I have to start here because without you, I wouldn't be here...literally! First and foremost, thank you for knocking it out and giving birth to me. Thank you for encouraging me as a little girl that I could do anything I set my mind to. Thank you for not murdering me and hiding the body when I was a teenager and for dealing with all my crazy phases. Thank you for teaching me to always "keep on keeping on." Thank you for being you.

To Travis, my husband: Thank you for being the most incredible partner. Thank you for reminding me to lighten up and laugh when I get too serious. Thank you for loving me fiercely. Thank you for giving me two beautiful, incredible sons. You are such an amazing man, and I am so blessed to have you as my partner in this thing called life.

To my children: Thank you for making me a mother and for teaching me how to love someone more than I love myself. Thank you for all the lessons you teach me daily. What you have taught me about love, laughter, the power of curiosity, and patience (lots of lessons there!) guide me.

To my wolf pack: Thank you for all the memories, past and future. You ladies are my rocks, and I love you to the moon and back.

To Jonathon F: You were my first mentor in business, and you believed in me first (I still have no idea why!). I am forever grateful for how you helped me grow and for our friendship.

To Travis H: There are not enough words for how you have helped me grow. You keep me grounded and guided. Thank you for being an amazing partner in business and in friendship. Thank you for always being my biggest advocate.

To Kelly K: Thank you for taking a chance on me, and from day one helping me have a bigger vision. You have opened up more doors for me than I could possibly deserve.

To all my other friends and colleagues along the way: Thank you for everything. There are too many people who have shaped my life to possibly be able to thank you all, but please know you are all so important to me. What I have learned from all my experiences with you, whether positive or negative, has shaped me into the person I am today. I am so grateful for my life and for the contribution you have made to it.

Table of Contents

Chapter 1: Why We Must Control Our Thoughts 1

Chapter 2: Create a Vision That Gives You Maniacal Drive 33

Chapter 3: Mental Toughness 61

Chapter 4: Deliberate Creation: Prioritize Your Time 95

Chapter 5: Adopt a Routine to Stay Positive 103

Chapter 6: Connections 131

Chapter 7: Your Financial House 147

Chapter 8: Never Stop Learning 161

About the Author 167

CHAPTER 1
Why We Must Control Our Thoughts

"Happiness can be achieved through training the mind."

—The Dalai Lama

Meet Lucy—A Real Bitch

Meet Lucy. She is someone very close to me, although not a friend.

Lucy is constantly reminding me of *all* the things I do wrong. When I make a mistake, she is the first to chastise me. When I have a goal, Lucy tells me all the reasons why my goal is not going to be accomplished.

She puts me down constantly. She tells me when I look fat in a dress and when my hair looks out of place. She is quick to point out any other blemish I may have. Lucy doesn't support me and often tries to sabotage my efforts. When I wanted to get in shape, Lucy would encourage me to hit snooze and skip the gym, and she told me I should eat French fries instead of the salad I packed for lunch.

Lucy is a total bitch...and she lives in my head. I named her after Lucy van Pelt in the *Peanuts* comic series by Charles Schultz. That Lucy made her debut in newspapers on March 3, 1952. She was known around the neighborhood (and by her little brother, Linus) for being crabby and bossy. Still today, Lucy can often be found dispensing advice from her 5-cent psychiatrist's booth, yanking away Linus's security blanket, or humiliating Charlie Brown.[1]

Well, my Lucy used to be the boss. She was in total control of most of our conversations. But now I am in charge, and when Lucy tries to get loud, I have the tools to box that bitch—to put her in her place.

This book is about the lessons I have learned to shut

---

1. "Lucy," Peanuts.com, https://www.peanuts.com/characters/lucy/#.

her up. It's about brain science and how to make your brain work for you, not against you. It's about insight from those at the top of their game on how they practice mental toughness and defeat their gremlins. It's about how they silence that inner jerk in their minds.

If you have a Lucy, a Bob, an Alex—someone who is filling your head with fear, self-doubt, or anxiety—this book is for you. I hope you find the lessons I have learned valuable, and I hope they will empower you to get control of that bitch or son of a bitch in your head.

Everyone Has Negative Thoughts

You have negative thoughts that drag you down, and you're not the only one. You might think no one else struggles like you do—*especially* not the super-successful—but that's a lie. It's not just a *you* issue; it's an *everyone* issue. It's a *human* issue. Everyone has an inner jerk in his or her mind, demanding attention for gloom, doom, and negativity.

We look at people like Patrick Mahomes, Ariana Grande, and Satya Nadella and think that for them, achieving success must have been effortless. It seems like, for some people, things just come easily. I'm here to tell you that's bullshit. It wasn't effortless for them. Before their success came an intense amount of practice and even failure, and the same is true for you and me. The brain is the most complex organ in our bodies, and we must shape it by maintaining a positive mindset. That's how we make sure our minds work for us instead of against us.

In my line of work, part of my job is to develop financial professionals so they, in turn, can guide their clients with rock-solid financial principles. What I will share with you in this book has helped me become more confident as a leader in the financial world. But these lessons will be valuable to you, no matter what your field, your goals, or your position in your life's journey.

I encourage you to allow yourself to be open to new concepts as you read this book. There might be some topics you'll have a knee-jerk reaction to. At my speaking engagements, sometimes people are skeptical at first. There are some concepts that seem a little "hocus-pocus" to them. Trust me here. Just be open. These concepts *will* yield results.

I know this from personal experience.

My Story

I grew up in Palm Springs, California, an only child.

Even though I had a charmed childhood for the most part, Lucy, that bitch, began filling my mind with doubt and fear early on.

I was somewhat of a badass when I was a kid. I was a tomboy. I took taekwondo from the ages of nine to sixteen. I achieved a black belt when I was just twelve. The final test to earn my black belt was to fight four adults at the same time. My instructor at the time, Master Aleem, didn't care that I was just twelve. We all went through the same test, and it was time for me to prove I had the courage, skills, and fight in me to join the elite ranks that so few achieve. I remember putting my back against a wall so my four opponents couldn't get me from behind. They could only come at me from the front and the sides.

I'm sure it was tough for my parents to see their twelve-year-old getting pummeled by four people. But they knew I was tough, and they kept shouting at me to remind me I was tough.

During that fight, I was exhausted. I couldn't breathe. I felt like I was going to suffocate. I was in pain, and the voice in my mind—Lucy—kept telling me to just lie down and curl up in a ball, and they would call off the test. Lucy had good intentions. She was trying to keep me safe. Your brain attempts to create safety, comfort, and stability for you. But I didn't join taekwondo to be comfortable. I joined to grow.

In those moments in life, when you have your back against the wall, and your opponents are coming at you, you have to make a decision: "Do I curl up into a ball and let them, or life, keep pummeling me? Or do I fight with every last breath I have?"

I chose to fight that day and proudly earned my black belt.

Lucy had good intentions in trying to keep me safe. But in doing so, she sabotaged my confidence and filled my mind with negative thoughts. The fact that I was a taekwondo badass didn't stop Lucy from trying to take me down.

All through school, Lucy would tell me I wasn't good enough, brave enough, or smart enough to succeed. Our constant banter had me questioning everything in life, including my path for my future. I really struggled to identify what I wanted to be when I grew up. I did love theatre, though, and I participated in theatre when I was in high school. My favorite role was production manager. I had dreams of going into production professionally. I wanted to work in Hollywood.

But when I was a senior, my guidance counselor told me, "Misty, you're too smart for Hollywood. What you're really good at is math. You have to go into math."

I *was* really good at math. I was at the top of my class in AP calculus, algebra, and physics. But it wasn't my passion.

Once I got to college, I dropped out four times. I couldn't make up my mind about what I wanted to do, so I kept dropping out, re-enlisting, dropping out, re-enlisting. And with each re-enlistment, I'd choose a different major. Each time I gave up on a major, Lucy worked hard to keep me feeling defeated by reminding me only "losers" dropped out of college, and I was tracking to be a Loser with a capital L. I listened to her back then because I didn't know how to make her go away.

Eventually, Lucy convinced me I was never going to get it right on my own, so I should just follow my high-school counselor's advice. Instead of pursuing production in Hollywood, I got a finance degree. I had no idea what I wanted to do with a finance degree, but there I was, with one in hand. I landed in the financial services industry as a financial advisor.

After a few years of building a practice as a financial advisor with a team, I was promoted into management in 2012. Today I am a Managing Partner, co-leading an organization with four other partners in seven different states. In this role, I am responsible for new-talent acquisition and development for our firm. I love what I do, and I feel grateful daily for my life. But the road was not easy...

When I was making a huge transition in 2012, from being a financial advisor at the firm where I had begun my career to taking on the role of Managing Director at my current firm, I was two months newly engaged. My then-fiancé and I had just bought our first house a month before (which we had no idea how we were going to afford), and I had just left the comfort and familiarity of the only firm I had ever known. If you look up the top ten most stressful things you can do in life, switching jobs, buying or remodeling a home, and getting married all make the list—and I decided to do all three in the space of a couple of months! Go big or go home, right?

Terror set in. More people than I care to remember were rooting against me, telling me I didn't have the skill set to make it in the role I'd been hired for. Lucy was right there with them, chiming in, her voice loud and strong, filling my head with fear, self-doubt, trash talk, and reasons why this or that *won't* work instead of why it will, why it *must*.

I believed they were right. There was no way this green, twenty-something girl, who was the first in her family to go to college, could be successful. There were endless

sleepless nights filled with worry, anxiety, and fear. Feelings of inadequacy, battles with imposter syndrome, and the occasional bout of uncontrollable tears. I didn't know it at the time, but Lucy was the puppet master, controlling the strings of my negative emotions. I had mastered the art of physical battle as a black belt in taekwondo, but I was a white belt—a novice—when it came to understanding the mental battle.

It took me a lot of time, learning, and effort to realize that it was up to me to box that bitch, Lucy.

I feel incredibly fortunate that in my industry, professional development and continued education are encouraged and celebrated. Being in my business for more than a decade, I have had the privilege of going to many conferences about growth and how to take your practice to the next level. It was during these conferences that I started learning about the human brain and how powerful it is. I learned that the power can work for you and help you achieve success beyond your wildest dreams. But it can also sabotage you, paralyze you, and cut you down at your knees before you even get started.

I learned that *I* am the only one who can take control of my thoughts and to turn the negative thoughts into positive ones. If we listen to Lucy and to all the people around us who are filling our brains with gunk, we will never become the best version of ourselves.

Me—Write a Book?!

Writing a book was never a major life goal of mine. I love reading and am constantly reading or listening to other people's books (I shoot for two or three per month). But writing my own book was never front of mind for me. I have focused most of my time on my career and my family.

Through the years, many people have suggested to me that if I wanted to up my game in business, I needed to write a book. But I really didn't want to. I have been too busy running my business, helping my husband run his business, and chasing around my two small kids, Jax and Ryder.

At this stage in my life, I rarely get the opportunity to pee without being interrupted—literally. People at my office follow me to the bathroom with "Got a minute?" questions, and anyone with children knows there is absolutely no privacy in the bathroom at home. So if I can't poop and pee in peace, there is certainly no f'ing time to write a book!

But then something changed in my mentality. Almost everyone I knew, in both my personal and professional life, was struggling. They were struggling with barriers that I knew they had set themselves. I would go to conferences and meet strangers, and they were all struggling, too. It seemed as though everyone I was interacting with was struggling in some form or another with issues that were caused by the fear, anxiety, or self-doubt that their minds fabricated.

Some were unable to accomplish their business goals. Others had trouble aligning well with their teams. And many were failing to hit their sales goals. Everyone seems to be struggling to accomplish the mountain of tasks in their daily lives.

Many people struggle with personal stuff, too. Maybe they don't communicate well with their spouse or their children. Maybe they are unable to lose the weight they have been desperately trying to get off. Or maybe they are not fulfilling their dream of (*insert dream here*).

I was struggling with all those things myself, and for years I had been working on ways to break through the barriers to accomplishing what I wanted. I read everything I could about how to be a peak performer, get rid of the mental blocks, and live a life of total fulfillment.

I found myself constantly sharing the things I had learned from my books. So I sat down and wrote this book about the concepts I have learned over the years that have been the most beneficial to me. These concepts have helped me evolve from a life of constant struggle to a life of great fulfillment. I started writing this book before the COVID-19 pandemic of 2020 disrupted our lives. As I watched those close to me and those around the world struggling to stay positive during this unprecedented time of uncertainty and change, I realized that the message in this book—we must choose to stay positive if we are to optimize our potential—is more relevant now than ever.

The pandemic did a number on people's mental health. Just three months into the pandemic, nearly half of Americans reported that the coronavirus crisis was harming their mental health, according to a Kaiser Family Foundation poll. A federal emergency hotline for people in emotional distress registered a more than 1,000 percent increase in April 2020 compared with the same time the previous year. And online therapy company Talkspace reported a 65 percent jump in clients from mid-February to early May 2020. Text messages and transcribed therapy sessions that the company collected anonymously showed that coronavirus-related anxiety was dominating patients' concerns.[2]

Also in April 2020, a survey by mental health provider Ginger revealed that during the pandemic, 88 percent of workers reported experiencing moderate to extreme stress over the previous four to six weeks. Seven of

---

2. "The Coronavirus Pandemic Is Pushing America into a Mental Health Crisis," William Wan, *The Washington Post*, May 4, 2020, https://www.washingtonpost.com/health/2020/05/04/mental-health-coronavirus/.

ten employees indicated that the COVID-19 pandemic was the most stressful time of their entire professional careers. Prescription provider Express Scripts reported that the pandemic led to a distinct rise in mental-health prescriptions that were previously on the decline.[3]

Mental toughness is a must on any normal day. Then when you add a pandemic to the mix, or some other life-altering catastrophe, it's harder than ever to survive, much less thrive. I'm right there with you as you navigate this crazy world.

If you get even one nugget from this book that helps you rise about your negative mind chatter, it will have been worth my time.

It's All in Our Minds

Our health, happiness, prosperity, and just about everything else starts in our minds. When people say, "It's all in your head," they're actually speaking the truth. To live our best lives—lives full of fulfillment—we must take control of our minds. Our mental state dictates our day-to-day happiness levels, our achievement levels, and our physical health.

Unfortunately, the opposite can also be true. Left to its own devices, your mind can make you feel incredibly unhappy. It can tear down your most important relationships, prevent you from achieving your life's goals,

---

3. Matthew Gavidia, "How Has COVID-19 Affected Mental Health, Severity of Stress Among Employees?" *The American Journal of Managed Care (AJMC)*, April 20, 2020, https://www.ajmc.com/newsroom/how-has-covid19-affected-mental-health-severity-of-stress-among-employees.

and make you physically ill.

A 2020 study from University College London found that obsessively worrying about the future or fixating on your problems could have serious ramifications for your future health. The study found a link between negative thinking and cognitive decline, as well as increased amounts of two proteins associated with Alzheimer's disease. Those negative thinking behaviors included continued worrying about the future and continual thinking about problems or emotions. The researchers found that people with more repetitive negative thinking patterns were more likely to have protein build-ups in their brains. Those same people also had higher rates of cognitive decline.[4]

We've got to change how we think.

Types of Negative Thinking

So just what types of negative thinking can derail our happiness and success? Here are just a few examples:

1. **Imposter syndrome:** This is when you suddenly think you're a fraud and that you have no business being successful—that you are an imposter, filling a role of leadership, maybe, but you're not worthy. I mentioned earlier that I have had boxing matches with imposter syndrome.

    This type of thinking is extremely common—

---

4. Shira Feder, "Negative Thinking Linked to Dementia Later in Life, Study Finds," msn.com, June 8, 2020, https://www.msn.com/en-us/health/medical/negative-thinking-linked-to-dementia-later-in-life-study-finds/ar-BB15cL8o.

an estimated 70 percent of people experience these impostor feelings at some point in their lives, according to an article published in the *International Journal of Behavioral Science*. When researchers first identified this type of thinking in 1978, they originally thought women were uniquely affected by it. But more recent research shows that anyone can have imposter syndrome; it can apply to anyone who isn't able to internalize and own their successes,[5]

Next time you do something you're proud of, acknowledge it to yourself. Recognize that you are making progress because of your efforts and talents, not just because of luck.

2. **Striving for perfection instead of excellence:** No one, and nothing, is perfect, so it's futile to waste valuable time and energy trying to achieve perfection. No one expects you to be perfect, even though that might be the message someone—maybe a parent, a teacher, or a coach—conveyed to you early in your life.

Psychotherapist Ilene Cohen, PhD, says people strive for perfection because they are looking for other people to give them worth; they rely on other people's opinions to give them a sense of their value. It's the same reason why people obsessively check how many "likes" or comments they receive after posting on Instagram or Twitter. Yet we must define our *own* worth; no one else can do it for us. She says,

---

5. "Yes, Impostor Syndrome Is Real. Here's How to Deal With It," Abigail Abrams, *TIME*, June 20, 2018, https://time.com/5312483/how-to-deal-with-impostor-syndrome/.

"Needing and lacking approval and acceptance will inevitably lead you to feel that what you do is never enough; you'll spend your life looking to do better and more." One tip Cohen suggests for banishing the need to be perfect is to learn to let go. She says, "Try to let go of whatever it is that's holding you back from accepting who you are...You aren't your pain, your past, or your emotions. It's usually negative ideas about ourselves and hurtful self-talk that get in the way of who we really want to be and push us to never make any mistakes."[6]

3. **All-or-nothing thinking:** This is when you think in extremes. You might think you're either a success or a failure, ignoring the vast spectrum of possibilities that lies between the two. All-or-nothing thinking is the most common type of *cognitive distortion*, which is an assumption we make based on minimal evidence, or without considering the evidence. This cognitive distortion can disrupt attempts to change behavior, such as sticking to a diet. If you think about your diet in all-or-nothing terms, it is likely that one indiscretion will derail all your effort. Remember, anything short of 100 percent might as well be 0 percent, so if you stick to your diet 90 percent of the time, all-or-nothing thinking will have you believe that you've totally failed, and that you might as well

---

6. "How to Let Go of the Need to Be Perfect," Ilene Strauss Cohen, PhD, *Psychology Today*, January 12, 2018, https://www.psychologytoday.com/us/blog/your-emotional-meter/201801/how-let-go-the-need-be-perfect.

eat whatever you want.[7]

If you make one mistake in a job interview, performance, audition, or something else, the reality is that you were spectacular for 95 percent of it, and the mistake composes only 5 percent of your entire effort. But too often, we focus only on the 5 percent and beat ourselves up for making mistakes. But everyone makes mistakes—in fact, we learn from our mistakes. We learn more from them than we do from our successes.

4. **Negative self-labeling:** I think most of us have done this. Maybe we trip over a bump in the sidewalk or misplace our keys, and then we begin berating ourselves, gritting our teeth, and whispering to ourselves, "You're so *stupid*!" or "You're so *clumsy*! What the eff is wrong with you?" Now, did you really deserve that tongue lashing for a simple mistake? No. Would you say that to someone you care about a lot if he or she did the same thing? Of course not! Treat yourself with compassion. Treat yourself like you would a loved one.

Grant Hilary Brenner, MD, is a psychiatrist and psychoanalyst. When he hears people giving themselves negative labels, he knows there are

---

7. "Cognitive Distortions: All-or-Nothing Thinking," Cognitive Behavioral Therapy Los Angeles, http://cogbtherapy.com/cbt-blog/cognitive-distortions-all-or-nothing-thinking.

reasons for that self-labeling. He says, "These words are easy to use, coming to mind in a jiffy, and often are what we heard growing up. They are words which offer quick fixes for complex problems and are accompanied by feelings of moral judgment, hatred, and utter rejection. Rather than understanding the nuance and creating bridges for understanding and communication, such labeling reflects underlying either–or thinking, generally fragmenting us apart from ourselves and each other in an act of linguistic violence."[8]

Ouch! Let's stop the self-inflicted linguistic violence. Seriously.

5. **Catastrophizing:** This is when you assume that the worst will happen. Often, it involves believing that you're in a worse situation than you really are or exaggerating the difficulties you face. Let's say you go on a date and have an amazing time. You and your date both leave feeling excited about your next encounter. The next day, you text that person to say how you are looking forward to seeing him or her again. Crickets. You don't get a text back. An hour goes by, then two, and then it's the entire day and you haven't heard back. Your mind starts spinning: "He/she doesn't like me and doesn't want to see me again. I am never going to find love." But in reality, your date's phone died, and he/she didn't have a charger and couldn't respond until he/she got home

---

8. "6 Hurtful Labels to Stop Using on Ourselves and Others," Grant Hilary Brenner, MD, *Psychology Today*, December 15, 2018, https://www.psychologytoday.com/us/blog/experimentations/201812/6-hurtful-labels-stop-using-ourselves-and-others.

and charged the phone. You jumped to the worst-case scenario when really, it was nothing. You can see how this type of negative thinking can be harmful to your psyche.

Research involving people who catastrophize and who also have chronic pain suggest they may have alterations in the hypothalamus and pituitary responses, as well as increased activity in the parts of the brain that register emotions associated with pain. People who have other conditions such as depression and anxiety, and people who are often fatigued, may also be more likely to catastrophize. A number of studies have suggested that mindfulness can treat or reduce catastrophizing.[9]

6. **Dwelling on the past:** This is when, even though a stressful event has passed and you know you can't change it or your response to it, you continue to think about it, dwell on it, and play it back in your mind over and over again.

Research indicates that stressful events with some sort of social component are more likely to stick with us than those events we experience alone. If we've had to perform in some way or another, we are then more likely to worry about others' negative judgment. Not only are we more likely to worry; we're also more likely to feel shame. It can become a vicious cycle. We have a stressful experience in public, we worry about how others will view how

---

9. "Catastrophizing: What You Need to Know to Stop Worrying," Healthline.com, https://www.healthline.com/health/anxiety/catastrophizing."

we acted, we feel ashamed of our actions (justified or not), and then we worry some more. The more shame we feel, the more likely we are to worry.[10]

Now that we've identified some of the types of negative thinking that rob us of vitality and confidence, let's look at just how harmful these negative thinking patterns are to our mental, and even our physical, health.

Dr. Caroline Leaf: Most Illness Is a Direct Result of Our Thoughts

According to Dr, Caroline Leaf, a world-renowned cognitive neuroscientist with a PhD in communication pathology (she's really smart), most physical illnesses that humans suffer from are a *direct* result of our thoughts. Dr. Leaf specializes in metacognitive and cognitive neuropsychology, and her work has been an incredible contribution to new discoveries around the power of our minds.

You sat down to read this book, so I am guessing you care about your health, your family, and your future and want to make positive changes in your life. If that's the case, then grab a glass of wine, or your beverage of choice, and keep reading. Understanding the functionality and power of our brains is incredibly important to that mission.

Now, focusing on the positive doesn't just help us become more successful; it's actually a critical ingredient in good physical and mental health.

---

10. "Why Do We Dwell in the Past?" Christy Matta, MA, PsychCentral, last updated July 8, 2018, https://psychcentral.com/blog/why-do-we-dwell-in-the-past/.

Since the early 1980s, Dr. Leaf has studied and researched the mind–brain connection. She says 75 to 95 percent of the illnesses that plague us today are a direct result of our thoughts. What we think about affects us significantly, both physically and emotionally.

Here is what Dr. Leaf says about the harm that can result from negative thoughts:

> It's an epidemic of toxic emotions. The average person has over 30,000 thoughts a day. Through an uncontrolled thought life, we create the conditions for illness; we make ourselves sick! Research shows that fear, all on its own, triggers more than 1,400 known physical and chemical responses and activates more than 30 different hormones.
>
> There are intellectual and medical reasons to forgive! Toxic waste generated by toxic thoughts causes the following illnesses: diabetes, cancer, asthma, skin problems, and allergies, to name just a few. Consciously control your thought life, and start to detox your brain! Change in your thinking is essential to detox the brain. Consciously controlling your thought life means not letting thoughts rampage through your mind. It means learning to engage interactively with every single thought that you have, and to analyze it before you decide either to accept or reject it.[11]

---

11. Dr. Caroline Leaf, "Controlling Your Toxic Thoughts," Dr. Leaf website, https://drleaf.com/about/toxic-thoughts/.

Dr. Leaf has spent the past thirty years developing a mind-based technique centered around the science of thoughts and memory formation to help people detox and rewire their brains. She says we can rewire our brains using her five-step process that takes only seven to sixteen minutes a day for twenty-one days.[12]

Enter Health Neuroscience: Physical and Mental Health Affect Each Other

Dr Leaf is not the only neuroscientist who is talking about these things. The connection between your physical health and the mind is so strong that an entire new field was created around it called "health neuroscience."

We often hear people talk as if physical health and mental health are two entirely separate conditions and that they have no effect on each other. But there is a lot of evidence to show that they affect each other in significant ways. So we need to take care of our mental health to help achieve good physical health, and vice versa.

In a 2015 study, a team of researchers from the University of Pittsburgh and Carnegie Mellon University explored what *health neuroscience* really is. They adopted the definition of *health* as the absence of physical or mental illness, disease, pain, or discomfort. The researchers distinguish physical health from mental health with the awareness that there are ambiguous boundaries, and significant parallels between, physical and mental health conditions (such as between cardiovascular disease

---

12. You can find details about Dr. Caroline Leaf's "21 Day Brain Detox" online program at www.21daybraindetox.com.

and depression), as well as clear physical, or biological, conditions that can lead to mental health issues.[13]

The fact that our mental health affects our physical health, and vice versa, is great news. It means that if we can gain control over our negative thoughts and improve our mental health, we can potentially improve our physical health. So if we're trapped in negative thinking, we can change it. We have to be aware of it first, and then we have to take steps to stop the negative tapes. That's what successful people do.

How Successful People Gain Control Over Their Minds

Successful people are masters at gaining cognitive control—in other words, controlling their thoughts. The first step is to identify and deal with anxiety. Even a tiny bit of stress disrupts our cognitive control.

Tony Ewing runs a business that uses behavioral analytics to help professionals and organizations identify, forecast, and address strategic challenges. He observes the habits of successful people to see where their behaviors overlap with proven insights from research. He has discovered that successful

---

13. Kirk I. Erickson, J. David Creswell, et al., "Health Neuroscience: Defining a New Field," US Department of Health and Human Services (HHS) Public Access, from Current Directions in Psychological Science, December 1, 2015, https://www.ncbi.nlm.nih.gov/pmc/articles/PMC4381930/

people stay calm amid stressful situations by doing things like distancing themselves from those situations and getting sufficient sleep. Another thing they do that's somewhat counterintuitive is, instead of trying to calm down in a turbulent situation, to get excited about the possibility of good things happening. Ewing notes that scientists from Harvard Business School found that because stress often stems from worrying that bad things will happen, forcing yourself to be calm just buries those thoughts, further building up stress. "A better response is to get excited about the possibility positive things will happen," he says. "In other words, within reason, getting excited about what good might come generates genuine calmness."[14]

OK, if you are still reading, then perhaps you buy in to the concept that it's important to control your thoughts. The challenging part is the fact that we are up against a massive opponent: the human mind. Our minds are powerhouses, and they're addicted to negativity.

"Negativity Bias" Hard-Wires Us to Focus on the Negative

Science tells us that it's typical for us to focus more on the negative than the positive. In fact, according to the National Science Foundation, 80 percent of our thoughts in any given day are negative! Eighty percent! And 95 percent of our thoughts are the same exact thoughts from

---

14. Tony Ewing, "7 Science-Backed Ways Successful People Stay Calm," *Forbes*, July 20, 2020, https://www.forbes.com/sites/tonyewing/2020/07/20/7-science-backed-ways-successful-people-stay-calm/#729976e74eee.

yesterday.[15] So basically, we just think the same negative crap, day in and day out. This isn't a good use of our time or energy!

This is why we tend to focus on bad news and emphasize negative possibilities more than positive outcomes. We are hard-wired that way. Psychologists call this phenomenon "negativity bias."

Nobel-prize winning researchers Kahneman and Tversky found that when making decisions, people consistently place greater weight on negative aspects of an event than they do on positive ones.[16] In fact, some researchers assert that negative emotions have an impact that's close to three times stronger than that of positive emotions.

Here's an example of negativity bias in action: You have an 8-hour workday, and 7.5 hours of the 8 were productive, engaging, and positive. But after one bad thirty-minute meeting, you leave the office feeling tired, defeated, and annoyed. Your spouse asks you at dinner how your day was, and all you can focus on is the negative thirty-minute engagement you had earlier.

According to Laura Mixon Camacho, PhD, a communication coach at Mixonian Institute, "The human brain remembers negative messages, results, and possibilities with greater magnitude than positive ones." The negativity bias served a strong evolutionary

---

15. Neringa Antanaityte, "Mind Matters: How to Effortlessly Have More Positive Thoughts," TLEX® Institute, https://tlexinstitute.com/how-to-effortlessly-have-more-positive-thoughts/.
16. Daniel Kahneman and Amos Tversky, "Choices, Values, and Frames," American Psychological Association, April 1984, https://psycnet.apa.org/doiLanding?doi=10.1037%2F0003-066X.39.4.341.

purpose. In pre-historic times, remaining alert for potential danger was the key to surviving. But, Camacho says, "Modern times favor humans who not only imagine a better future but who put in  the work to make it become reality. Fixating on negative possibilities creates harmful stress that actually shortens lifespans."[17]

So, although negativity bias may have served us well it the past, it doesn't serve us well now. We must work on deprogramming our brains from this natural bias.

This isn't a simple task, though. In fact, trying so hard to eliminate our negative thinking might be contributing to some of our unhappiness in the process. In his book *The Antidote: Happiness for People Who Can't Stand Positive Thinking*, journalist Oliver Burkeman notes that plenty of religious leaders, psychologists, and philosophers teach "that the effort to try to feel happy is often precisely the thing that makes us miserable. And that it is our constant efforts to eliminate the negative—insecurity, uncertainty, failure, or sadness—that cause us to feel so insecure, anxious, uncertain, or unhappy."[18]

---

17. Laura Camacho, "Four Ways Negativity Bias Slows You Down (And How To Stop It)," *Forbes*, February 26, 2019, https://www.forbes.com/sites/forbescoachescouncil/2019/02/26/four-ways-negativity-bias-slows-you-down-and-how-to-stop-it/#50de40d4c5f9.
18. Oliver Burkeman, The Antidote: Happiness for People Who Can't Stand Positive Thinking (New York: Farrar, Straus and Giroux, 2013), 13.

You might be thinking, "OK, Misty. First you say that being negative makes us sick and unhappy, so we should stop thinking negatively. Now you are suggesting that trying to stop thinking negatively contributes to our unhappiness. What the heck?"

There is a potential solution to this conundrum. Burkeman explains that the Stoics—philosophers of ancient Greece—had a way of dealing with possible misfortune: they practiced what they called "the premeditation of evils." "Rather than struggling to *avoid* all thought of these worst-case scenarios," Burkeman writes, "they counsel *actively dwelling* on them, staring them in the face."[19]

So it's not that we have to completely *stop* the negative thoughts from coming up. In fact, I would argue that it's almost impossible to do so. I call bullshit on any human being who tells you his or her thoughts are filled only with positivity, sunshine, and rainbows. But through our mental training, we can lessen the occurrences of negative thoughts. And when they do show up, we can acknowledge them for what they are and address them head-on.

When we use this kind of thinking—when we say to ourselves, "What is the absolute worst thing that could happen?"—we realize that the absolute worst isn't deadly.

For example, during the COVID-19 pandemic of 2020, many people feared losing their jobs. OK, let's say you do lose your job. What's the absolute worst thing that could happen? You will go on unemployment, and if that isn't

---

19. Ibid., 42.

enough money to meet your expenses, you could get a roommate. Our worst fear is usually, "I'm going to be homeless," but the reality is that we can move in with our parents or get a roommate.

It's unlikely that we will become homeless. If we just give ourselves that space and time to think about the situation, it really does help. Say to yourself: "OK, worst-case scenario. If (*fill in the blank*) happens, what next?" Then, when things *do* come to pass, we're relieved that (in most cases), the absolute worst didn't happen, after all.

That's a great way to box that bitch who's filling your brain with negative thoughts.

Psychologist Rick Hanson simplifies "negativity bias" by explaining it like this: "The brain is like Velcro for negative experiences but Teflon for positive ones." He says animals, including humans, generally learn faster from pain than pleasure. Again, it's a survival mechanism. Hanson says, "To keep our ancestors alive, Mother Nature evolved a brain that routinely tricked them into making three mistakes: *overestimating threats*, *underestimating opportunities*, and *underestimating resources* (for dealing with threats and fulfilling opportunities). This is a great way to pass on gene copies, but a lousy way to promote quality of life."[20]

Simply recognizing that your mind is automatically going to put more weight on the negative than the positive can help you overcome the constant barrage of incoming negativity. When someone seems to frown at you, don't

---

20. Rick Hanson, PhD, "Confronting the Negativity Bias," RickHanson.net, https://www.rickhanson.net/how-your-brain-makes-you-easily-intimidated/.

automatically assume that the person is unhappy with you. Maybe that person just got a speeding ticket or found out his kid needed surgery. Don't let self-doubt run amok before you know the facts.

I run across plenty of people who are weighed down with constant self-doubt. Working in consulting, a lot of times, I find that people take things really personally. They focus on the negative aspects of their daily interactions.

A client doesn't call one of my consultants back, and then, all of a sudden, his brain starts going haywire. He freaks out: "Oh, I've lost this client!" or "I did something wrong!" or "I shouldn't have said the thing I said at the last meeting!" (This is an example of *catastrophizing*, which we discussed in chapter 1.)

What really happened, of course, was that the client didn't call back because she had the flu or had to fly out to visit her sick mother or had a crazy deadline at work that took priority. But this happens all the time—our brains jump straight to the worst possible scenario.

We all need to work on stopping that! Stop the constant loop of negative tapes. Stop the shit from controlling our minds.

Pandemic Panic

During the COVID-19 pandemic of 2020, negativity bias was alive and well. Millions of people lost their jobs. Schools, businesses, gyms, parks, restaurants, and bars shut down. Social distancing created an unprecedented wave of loneliness. Stay-at-home orders forced individuals, couples, and families to be sequestered in their homes 24/7, unable to get out and do the things they enjoyed.

All that frustration was compounded when some states mandated that people wear face masks in public. In some cases, arguments about this mandate resulted in violence worldwide. This devastating situation was further complicated by the social unrest following the death of a black man, George Floyd, at the hands of a white police officer, along with the anxiety leading up to the 2020 presidential election.

Now, you might think that people would seek out positive and uplifting information during such a stressful time that dragged on and on. But just the opposite happened: people became somewhat obsessed with bad news and then felt even worse than they did before as they read one dreadful news story after another. It was so bad that a new term was coined to describe this obsessive dive into negative news headlines: *doomscrolling*.

Dr. Amelia Aldao, a clinical psychologist, warns that doomscrolling traps us in a "vicious cycle of negativity" that fuels our anxiety. "Our minds are wired to look out for threats," she says. "The more time we spend scrolling, the more we find those dangers, the more we get sucked into them, the more anxious we get." That grim content can then throw a dark filter over how you see the world, she explains. "Now you look around yourself, and everything feels gloomy, everything makes you anxious. So you go back to look for more information." And the cycle continues.[21]

Aldao is the director of Together CBT, a clinic that specializes in cognitive behavioral therapy. She has worked with her patients to cut back on doomscrolling. She encourages them to set a limit on the amount of time they scroll through news stories and to replace that activity with more positive activities like connecting with friends and sending funny stories to them.

Better yet, why not just stop watching and reading the negative news altogether?

Stop the Caca

All that negativity is just shit you don't need to pour into your head that's already filled with its own caca. *Caca* is the Spanish word for "shit." It also stands for "Crappy Attitude Causing Actions." If you don't control your thoughts, you probably will never reach your optimum level of potential and happiness. And we already covered the serious health problems that can result if we don't.

Silencing your inner jerk—boxing that bitch—is necessary if you want to be healthy, productive, and happy. But the question becomes, how do you do it? How do you stop your Lucy from flinging shit at you on a daily basis?

---

21. Lulu Garcia-Navarro, "Your 'Doomscrolling' Breeds Anxiety. Here's How to Stop the Cycle," National Public Radio, July 19, 2020, https://www.npr.org/2020/07/19/892728595/your-doomscrolling-breeds-anxiety-here-s-how-to-stop-the-cycle.

Now that I've explained *why* it's important to keep a positive mindset, I want to offer some tips on *how* to do that. A great place to start is to create a compelling personal and/or business vision that will fuel maniacal drive. That's the focus of chapter 2.

CHAPTER 2

Create a Vision That Gives You Maniacal Drive

> "Drive is the engine of accomplishment. It allows a person to achieve whatever goals they set in life."
>
> —Barry Lubetkin, Clinical Psychologist

Maniacal Drive

When you are inspired to move forward and claim all that life has to offer you, I like to call that process "maniacal drive."

To me, *drive* is "intense motivation." It's passion. It's perseverance. It's determination. Drive is essential to our success, but how do we attain it?

Maybe you've read Stephen Covey's book *The 7 Habits of Highly Effective People*. Although I find the book a tough read, I love his concept of "beginning with the end in mind." Covey says that beginning with the end in mind means "to begin today with the image, picture, or paradigm of the end of your life as your frame of reference or the criterion by which everything else is examined."[22] It's knowing exactly where you want to go.

This concept has been such an important part of my own journey. How do you get where you're going if you don't know where you want to go?

---

22. Stephen R. Covey, *The 7 Habits of Highly Effective People* (New York: Free Press, 1989), 133.

By creating a compelling *vision* and then ensuring that every single decision you make, both in life and business, aligns with that vision.

Every coach I've ever had has started our work together by having me establish my vision. It serves as the foundation for everything else in my life.

Your *vision* is your mental picture of where you want to go. It is built around your *values*. My values are as follows:

- Never stop learning.
- Be kind to everyone.
- Live a life of stewardship by giving more to the world than you take.
- Love deeply and passionately.
- Laugh—a lot.
- Take care of your body; it's the only vessel you have to carry out your life's mission.

Are you clear on your values? We experience greater fulfillment in life when we live by our values. Our values represent what we stand for and help guide our behavior. There are many resources, including entire books, on creating values statements, but I have listed some core values on the next page to help guide your thinking. Which words resonate with you?

Circle the ones that jump out at you, or jot down others that this list prompts you to think of.

Acceptance	Devotion	Humor	Satisfaction
Accomplishment	Dignity	Independence	Self-reliance
Altruism	Discipline	Innovation	Selflessness
Ambition	Drive	Inspiration	Sensitivity
Awareness	Effectiveness	Integrity	Serenity
Balance	Empathy	Intelligence	Service
Beauty	Empowerment	Joy	Significance
Boldness	Energy	Justice	Smarts
Bravery	Equality	Kindness	Spirit
Brilliance	Ethics	Knowledge	Spontaneity
Calmness	Excellence	Leadership	Stability
Candor	Experience	Love	Stewardship
Carefulness	Family	Loyalty	Strength
Challenge	Fearlessness	Motivation	Sustainability
Charity	Fidelity	Openness	Teamwork
Comfort	Focus	Optimism	Thankfulness
Community	Foresight	Passion	Thoroughness
Compassion	Fortitude	Patience	Thoughtfulness
Confidence	Freedom	Peace	Timeliness
Connection	Friendship	Performance	Transparency
Consciousness	Fun	Persistence	Truth
Contribution	Generosity	Playfulness	Understanding
Conviction	Goodness	Poise	Unity
Courage	Grace	Power	Vision
Creation	Gratitude	Being present	Vitality
Creativity	Greatness	Prosperity	Wealth
Curiosity	Happiness	Purpose	Winning
Decisiveness	Hard work	Reflection	Wisdom
Dedication	Harmony	Respect	Wonder
Dependability	Health	Responsibility	
Determination	Honesty	Results	
Development	Humility	Rigor	

Once you have identified your values, they will help guide your vision.

Write Your Own Eulogy to Discover Your Vision

Vision is what you want to happen in the future. If you don't know what you want out of life, how can you spend your time and effort making it happen? You have to be intentional about bringing your vision to life.

Many people don't seem to have a vision. You ask them what they want out of life, and their answers are vague, at best. In my work, I have interviewed hundreds of people who were exploring a career with our firm, and this is always one of the first questions I ask them. The typical answers I get are "I don't know" or "I haven't really given that much thought." People are just going through life on autopilot, without any real ideas for their future.

I discovered a great way to figure out my personal vision through one of the leadership courses I took. One of the exercises assigned through the course was to write my own eulogy. The purpose of this exercise is to figure out what we want people to say about us when we die. Doing that makes you take a really good, hard look in the mirror and say, "Am I living my life in a way that will lead people to say these things about me that I'd love for them to say?"

If the answer is no, then something has to change.

Here is the eulogy I wrote for myself, worded as though my husband is delivering it at my funeral:

My Eulogy

I'm overwhelmed, but not surprised, at how many people are here with us to celebrate Misty's life. As you can see by looking around the room, she made an impact on all of us. To say that she was a people person is an understatement. She had a passion for people, young and old, and truly believed there was value in everyone. She made friends wherever we went. There were often times that we were out to dinner, and she would go into the restroom and come out with a new friend.

She had a drive about her that was enviable. She excelled in every aspect of her life, from the sports she played to her work life. She loved what she did for a living, and for her, it wasn't a job, or even a career—it was a calling. She was warm and inviting at work, but she also meant business. She held herself and everyone on her team accountable to high expectations, and that's why she was so successful.

She was smart, ambitious, and hard-working, but she was committed to playing just as hard as she worked.

From skydiving to whitewater rafting, we tried it all together. She loved to travel, as most people do, but she traveled differently. She immersed herself in the culture and took the time to study the customs in the places we visited—to really meet the people, learn their stories. She had a passion for life, and her energy was contagious. She was kindhearted and charitable, and she made it her mission to give back to the world more than she took. If it were up to her, she would have adopted every single stray dog on the planet.

Misty loved her family as much as she loved her work and hobbies, and man, we were one hell of a team. We had a relationship that most people thought existed only in Hollywood. She could light up any room she walked into, and she lit up my world the day I met her. I knew the first second I saw her that I would marry her one day, and I was lucky enough that she picked me. It didn't matter how stressful of a day she had at the office, or what negativity was going on around us—whenever we were together, everything was perfect. She knew how to make all the worries disappear in our moments together.

She was an amazing wife and an even better mother. She taught our boys to be strong, hardworking, and driven, but also kind, loving, and generous. She was present for them daily and was a rock for them to lean on in life.

We will miss her greatly, but we know she's just on another traveling adventure, meeting people from the history of the world, probably karaokeing for them her best rendition of "Bust a Move."

I know many of you have probably been thinking that this has been a very unconventional funeral. Misty made me promise that there would be no "Amazing Grace" playing, no sad songs whatsoever. She wanted this day to be as fun as she was: open bar, AC/DC, reminiscing about fun memories, and of course a photo booth with silly props to remember the celebration. So with that said, thank you for coming, and let's get this party started.

I highly recommend doing this exercise. I know it feels weird to write your own eulogy, but it can help you figure out what you ultimately want to accomplish in life. When you realize what type of legacy you want to leave and how you want people to remember you, then you will be more intentional about living your life in a way that lives up to that legacy.

Now it's time to write your own eulogy. How do you want people to remember you? How were your relationships? Is the room at the funeral home empty, or is it full of people you touched and inspired or impacted? What kind of impact did you have on people's lives? What do you want your legacy to be? Write your eulogy with a vision in your mind of what you want people to say about you once you're gone—and then live in a way that will fulfill that vision.

Your Eulogy

The eulogy exercise, coupled with your values statement, is a great focus for how you want to lead your life. But it is also important to break down your goals and vision into more tangible, manageable timelines. I love to design personal and business vision statements that take me out three to five years into the future. It's far enough into the future to give me big, exciting things to strive for, but not so far out that it doesn't feel real.

Is It Your Vision, or Someone Else's?

Truly understanding your vision is vital. When putting together your vision, one of the first questions to ask yourself is, "Is it really *my* vision?"

Are you fully bought in, or did someone else hand you the vision they think is right for you? So often, we set goals based on what we think society says we should have, or what the company manager tells us to strive for, or what our parents or spouse said we should do.

But what do *you* want your career, your future, your life to look like? Spend some time digesting that question. Think about what your life would look like if it were a blank canvas, and you could paint on it whatever you wanted. What does your vision look like?

Once you find it, devote your unwavering commitment to get there. Do whatever it takes to see that vision through. Develop a maniacal drive. Every time you have to make a decision, ask yourself if it supports and gets you closer to your vision. Spend time and effort doing *only* the things that support you in reaching your vision.

What Do You Love, and Why?

Often, I meet people who, after working in their career field for twenty or thirty years, say, "You know, I always wanted to go into finance, but I never did because (*fill in the blank*)." Usually, that blank is filled with someone having told them they shouldn't pursue finance, or their own doubts about themselves.

Find your personal vision, and build it up. If your vision is strong enough, you won't have to be pushed toward it. It will pull you. It will fuel your maniacal drive!

Oprah famously said, "Create the highest, grandest vision possible for your life because you become what you believe."

For me, that vision includes having a career in which I know I make a difference every single day. It's having an office full of people I love, people I'm excited to work with. It's having an incredible team who supports my efforts so I can also have an abundance of quality time with my family. It's having an income that allows me to support my family and travel all over the world, while also being able to give back and make a difference in my community and to worldwide causes that resonate with me, like those having to do with children and hunger. It's having amazing health and energy so I can be there to play with my children. It's having deep relationships and sharing a fierce love with my husband.

What do you want your future to look like? What is your "grandest vision possible"?

Early in my career, I was fortunate enough to meet former NFL player and coach Tony Dungy in person. He often talks about the power of vision. He said, "The first step toward creating an improved future is developing the ability to envision it. Vision will ignite the fire of passion that fuels our commitment to do whatever it takes to achieve excellence. Only vision allows us to transform dreams of greatness into the reality of achievement through human action. Vision has no boundaries and knows no limits. Our vision is what we become in life."

What Are Your Priorities?

To have a clear vision, you need to know what's more important to you than anything else. Often, we say something is important to us, but the way we live our lives proves otherwise. To find out which areas of your life need some attention, assess yourself using this pie diagram:

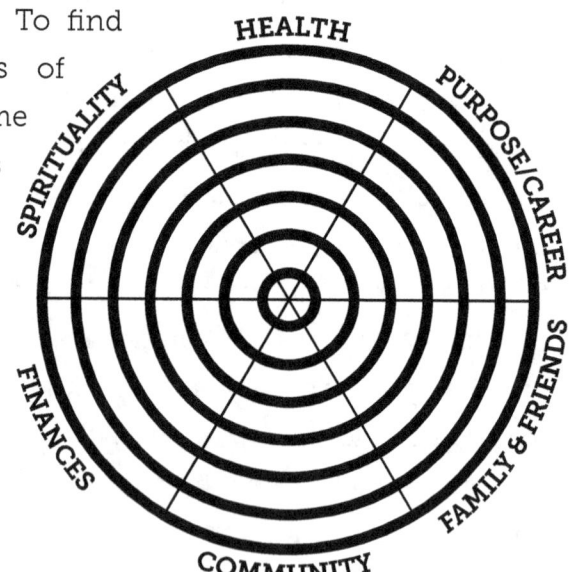

In the diagram, grade yourself on a scale of 1 to 7 on how successful you feel you are in each category of your life:

1. Health (mental and physical)
2. Purpose/career
3. Your relationships with your family and friends
4. Involvement in your community
5. Finances
6. Spirituality

Just shade in the pie from the inner corner to the outer edges according to the grade you gave yourself for each category. For example, if you rate yourself a 3 in the health category, shade in three lines.

This is what my pie looked like the first time I did this exercise:

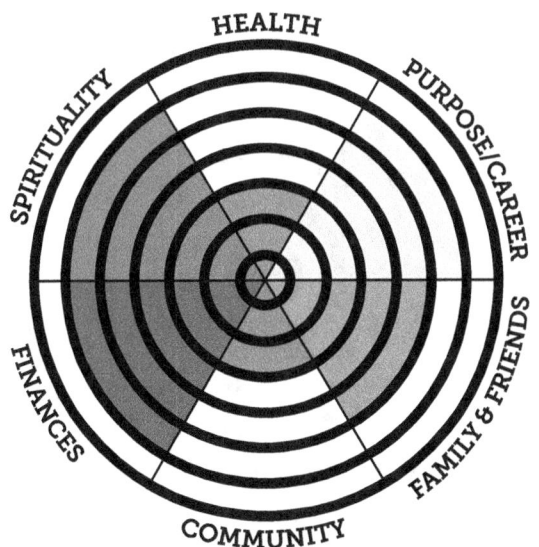

For me, this was a powerful visual. When I first saw it, it hit me in the face. Lucy was like, "Whoa, holy crap! You suck at certain areas of your life."

Seeing that wonky shape helped me realize I was doing great from a career and financial perspective. But I was seriously lacking in taking care of my health, and I wasn't as involved in my community as I wanted to be.

I was making a great living. My balance sheet was healthy. But I was thirty pounds overweight, I wasn't spending enough quality time with my kids, and I wasn't going on enough date nights with my husband. And, while I was giving financially to the community, I wasn't involved the way I wanted to be.

This exercise won't mean anything unless you actually shade in the pie yourself. So here is a blank version of the diagram again. Happy shading!

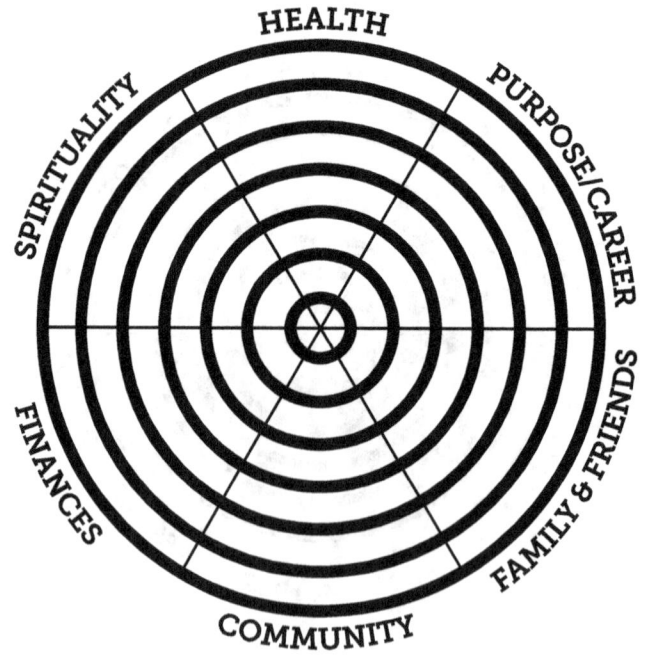

After you fill in your pie and reflect on where you stand, it's time to figure out what your perfect 7—your completely filled-in pie—looks like in practical terms. What do you want your life to look like spiritually? Financially? What does your ideal physical and mental health look like? What would pure success in your career look like? How active would you like to be in your community?

Take some time to write down how you want your life to look in each category...but write it in the *present tense*. Write it as though you've already accomplished it. It might feel strange or silly, but it is exactly what your brain needs.

So, instead of saying "I want to earn a hundred thousand dollars a year," write down "*I make* a hundred thousand dollars a year." You've got to tell your brain that these things have already happened.

Brain studies reveal that thoughts actually produce the same mental instructions as actions. Mental imagery impacts many cognitive processes in the brain: motor control, attention, perception, planning, and memory. So the brain is getting trained for actual performance during visualization. It's been found that mental practices can enhance motivation, increase confidence, improve motor performance, prime your brain for success, and increase states of flow.[23]

Jot down some points about what you would like each area of your life to be like:

---

23. A. J. Adams, "Seeing Is Believing: The Power of Visualization," *Psychology Today*, December 3, 2009, https://www.psychologytoday.com/us/blog/flourish/200912/seeing-is-believing-the-power-visualization.

1. In the area of mental and physical health, I
   _____
   _____
   _____

2. In the area of purpose/career, I
   _____
   _____
   _____

3. In terms of my relationships with my family and friends, I
   _____
   _____
   _____

4. In terms of involvement in my community, I
   _____
   _____
   _____

5. In the area of finances, I
   _____
   _____
   _____

6. In the area of spirituality, I
   _____
   _____
   _____

Now that you have taken some time to think through each area of your life, put it all together, and write your vision in a cohesive statement that will guide every decision you make:

_____

_____

_____

_____

_____

_____

_____

_____

_____

_____

_____

_____

_____

_____

_____

_____

_____

_____

This isn't necessarily a quick exercise; it took me at least a couple of days to sketch out my perfect life. Take your time, and put some thought into it. Then, once you have your clear vision in front of you, all you've got to do is make it your obsession! This is where maniacal drive comes in—complete dedication to achieving success in these areas. Failure is not an option.

This is powerful! All this, just from your thoughts.

Written Goals Are a Must for Achieving Success

There is intention for why I provided room for you to actually write out the exercises in this book. Written goals are much more powerful than just keeping it all in your head. For optimum effect, state your priorities in terms of goals you want to reach. Goal setting is one of the hallmarks of many wealthy and successful people.

But it's estimated that less than 3 percent of people have goals that are written down.[24]

To accomplish bodacious things in life, you need to set goals, and you need to write them down. *Goals keep you connected to your vision*, and that's important. When your goals are front of mind, that day-to-day grind won't keep you from forgetting what's most important to you.

---

24. "Success Through Goal Setting," Part 1 of 3, Brian Tracy International, https://www.briantracy.com/blog/personal-success/success-through-goal-setting-part-1-of-3/.

Mark Murphy, who founded www.LeadershipIQ.com, conducted a study and found that fewer than 20 percent of people could state that their goal was "so vividly described in written form (including pictures, photos, drawings, etc.)" that they could literally show it to other people, and they would know exactly what the person was trying to achieve."[25]

Murphy says that vividly describing your goals in written form is strongly associated with goal success. People who very vividly describe or picture their goals are anywhere from 1.2 to 1.4 times more likely to successfully accomplish their goals than people who don't.[26] That means they are 120 to 140 percent more likely to accomplish their goals, simply by visualizing their goals! That's a pretty big difference in goal achievement just from writing your goals on a piece of paper.

Writing your goals down helps on two levels, according to Murphy:[27]

1. **External storage**—When you write your goals down, you are storing that information in a location that is very easy to access and review at any time. You'll remember something much better if you're staring at a visual cue (reminder) every single day.

---

25. Mark Murphy, "Neuroscience Explains Why You Need to Write Down Your Goals if You Actually Want to Achieve Them," *Forbes*, April 15, 2018, https://www.forbes.com/sites/markmurphy/2018/04/15/neuroscience-explains-why-you-need-to-write-down-your-goals-if-you-actually-want-to-achieve-them/#27bb8c187905.
26. Ibid.
27. Ibid.

2. **Encoding**—*Encoding* is the biological process by which the things we perceive travel to our brain's hippocampus, where they're analyzed. From there, decisions are made about what gets stored in our long-term memory and what gets discarded. Writing improves that encoding process. When you write your goal down, you have a much greater chance of remembering it.

Review your goals every morning and every night. You have to start your day making sure you're paying attention to your goals. And then you need to end your day by asking yourself, "How much progress did I make on my goals today?"

Focusing on your goals at least twice a day will give you maniacal drive because it causes you to think about them all the time. This is true in your personal life as well as in your business life.

My husband and I set family goals at least once per year. We discuss what we want to accomplish as a family unit, whether it's a financial goal, a vacation we want to take, or a piece of real estate we want to buy. We decide on those goals as a team, and then we work toward them as a team. Working on goals with someone else increases your focus on them and infuses the process of reaching those goals with extra passion and power!

I have seen people spend hours and hours creating a business plan. And then four months later, I'll ask them how they're doing on their business plan, and they can't even remember what was in it because they never looked at it.

A lot of people attempt to set goals by setting New Year's resolutions. But that isn't a winning proposition. About 80 percent of people fail to stick to their New Year's resolutions for longer than six weeks.[28] I believe it's because people set resolutions that are too broad, and they don't incorporate those goals into their daily planning. It's kind of like a friend asks, "Hey, what are your New Year's resolutions?" over that tenth shot of tequila at a New Year's Eve party. So you make something up, shout it out, and never remember it again.

Once you've gotten crystal clear on your goals and vision, there are several tools that will help you keep them front and center in a highly visual format, so they become an even more powerful tool in helping you achieve success. I have learned many strategies for keeping my vision front and center so I can focus on it at all times. This can be as simple as putting reminders about your vision anywhere and everywhere: on the visor in your car, on your mirror, on your desk, in the drawer where you keep your secret stash of goodies, etc. Or you can go for a strategy that's a bit more involved. Let's look at a couple of options.

---

28. Lindsay Dodgson, "The Psychology Behind Why We're So Bad at Keeping New Year's Resolutions," Business Insider, January 7, 2018, https://www.businessinsider.com/the-psychology-behind-why-we-cant-keep-new-years-resolutions-2018-1.

Visual Tools to Keep Your Dreams Front of Mind

Here are several tools that will help you transform your dreams and aspirations into visible reminders and keep them front of mind.

1. Vision Boards

It's a lot of fun to create a vision board. Just get a bulletin board and post photos, quotes, and other reminders of your vision on it.

Jack Canfield, the originator of the ridiculously successful *Chicken Soup for the Soul* books, said this about vision boards: "The inspirational collages serve as your image of the future—a tangible example, idea, or representation of where you are going. They should represent your dreams, your goals, and your ideal life."[29]

I love vision boards so much that I have two of them. They sit on my dresser. I see them every morning when I wake up and every night before I go to bed. They remind me about my purpose and what I want to accomplish as I start and end each day.

Include on your vision board pictures, words, and phrases that represent your ideal life in each of the six categories on the pie diagram you filled in. Traditionally, these things are cut from magazines and glued onto the board, but you can find images in other places, too, and you can write whatever words you want on the board yourself. Here are some ideas for images to use, to get you started:

---

29. Jack Canfield, "Vision Board Ideas and How to Make Yours Better | Jack Canfield." Jack Canfield, January 2, 2019, https://www.jackcanfield.com/blog/how-to-create-an-empowering-vision-book/.

- A person with a fit body on a morning run
- A beautiful house
- Smooth river pebbles stacked gracefully on top of each other
- A couple holding hands
- A person walking the streets of Paris
- The Taj Mahal
- Healthy food
- A happy family playing together at the park
- A mountain biker hitting the trails
- A confident public speaker
- A nonprofit organization's work in the field
- A private, in-ground pool

Here are some examples of words and phrases you might want to include:

- Good vibes
- Strong is sexy
- Zero debt
- Unstoppable
- Success
- Breathe
- Live in the moment
- Read
- Family
- Love your body
- Money is no object
- Giving back
- Plant-based
- See the world

Google "vision board examples," and you'll find some great ideas. Go crazy—make it yours!

2. Mind Movies

You might be a millennial or Gen Z, and you're thinking, "Oh, my God, Misty, you're so old! No one does vision boards like that anymore." I hear you. You can create an electronic vision board using computer software or a mobile app, like Mind Movies. My business coach introduced me to this app, and it's my new obsession.

It's an app that enables you to create a video with pictures and affirmations that you choose. You can even set it to music. So I have essentially digitized my vision board into a music video, and I watch it every morning when I first wake up. Before I get out of bed, I am watching this thing.

Here is an image from my mind movie:

3. Index Cards

A third tool I use to make my vision visual is a set of index cards. It's a strategy I learned from a different business coach a few years ago. It's old-school, I know, but I have to say, it was one of the best tips I've ever gotten.

You attach visual images of your goals on 3" x 5" index cards, and they go everywhere in your world. I have these cards displayed on my bathroom mirror, on my refrigerator, in my car, and three in my office. As I walk around doing life, I look up and see these cards, and it causes me to pause and ask myself, "Am I working toward my vision? Is what I am doing right now the best thing to support me in my mission?"

As I accomplish my goals, I replace them with even bigger ones. This isn't a static, one-time exercise. I constantly strive for continual growth and better things in life. We must make the most of every moment we have.

We have 86,400 seconds in a day. It takes only *one* of those seconds to make a choice. These cards are a great reminder that I need to *choose* to focus on the things that are important to me.

The Law of Attraction

I know all this might sound like hocus-pocus, but the research and brain science out there suggest that it works. For instance, the law of attraction states that you tend to attract whatever you focus your thoughts and intentions on most strongly. It isn't "magic," and it's not New Age.

As Arizona State University psychology professor

Neil Farber puts it, the principle of attraction is "a social scientific phenomenon, which implies that you have an active role in this process—your positive attitude, beliefs, and behavior will most likely bring you more of the same."[30]

With every decision that crosses your path, ask yourself if it supports and gets you closer to your vision—and *only* do it if the answer is yes. This is *maniacal drive*, and it's your key to success.

It's what Michael Jordan was talking about when he said, "Some people want it to happen, some wish it would happen, others make it happen." And it's what Arnold Schwarzenegger meant when he said, "As long as the mind can envision the fact that you can do something, you can do it, as long as you really believe one hundred percent."

Now, we're human, and it's easy to get distracted because our lives are busy. This won't appeal to some people, but I had a business coach who had me wear a rubber band on my wrist for two weeks. Whenever I caught myself doing something that was taking me away from my vision, I'd snap myself with the rubber band. Ouch! That hurt. It's just a simple way to stay aware and focused on your goals. I do *not* walk around snapping myself with rubber bands in day-to-day life. But the exercise reinforced for me how consistent actions can train your mind.

Having a vision is critical, but without action, nothing is going to happen! You need to create a plan of action and activity that aligns with your vision and goals. The next step is to make it your obsession to make your vision come to

---

30. Neil Farber, "The Law of Attraction Revisited," *Psychology Today*, January 5, 2014, https://www.psychologytoday.com/us/blog/the-blame-game/201401/the-law-attraction-revisited.

life. I mean it—go after that vision like a zombie goes after brains. To do that, you must develop mental toughness to maintain your focus amid all the distractions flying at you.

People often tell me, "Oh, you're so put together, and you're so positive!" The truth is, without constantly focusing on my thoughts, I would be one of the most negative people out there. I practice *really hard* at making sure I correct the thoughts in my head before any words come out.

This concept of *practice* is extremely important. It doesn't just come to us effortlessly.

In fact, when I was a kid, I was known for telling people their hair was ugly or that I didn't like their shirt. My mom said I was super-embarrassing when I was a kid. Now that I'm an adult, those same critical thoughts sometimes cross my mind—usually about myself. But now I do a better job of making sure that I correct the thoughts in my head before any words come out. Again, I have to work at it. I have to *practice* either stifling my negative thoughts or replacing them with positive ones.

That's how we build *mental toughness*.

Mental toughness is absolutely necessary if you're going to shut out all those negative voices that are filling your mind with doubt and worry. You need mental toughness to move from building your vision to going after your vision and making it a reality. Without mental toughness, none of the other concepts matter.

But if you don't have mental toughness now, it's OK. You can develop it! It's not like you're either born with it or not.

Believing You Can Improve Is the First Step

Everyone experiences negative thoughts to different degrees. The more negative thoughts have eroded your confidence and beaten you down, the more important it is to turn that around. The first step in developing mental toughness is to *believe you can improve*.

One expert on this topic is Carol S. Dweck, PhD, who is the Lewis and Virginia Eaton Professor of Psychology at Stanford University.

More than thirty years ago, Dr. Dweck and her colleagues became interested in students' attitudes about failure. They noticed that some students rebounded, while other students seemed devastated by even the smallest setbacks. After studying the behavior of thousands of children, Dr. Dweck coined the terms *fixed mindset* and *growth mindset* to describe the underlying beliefs people have about learning and intelligence. When students believe they can get smarter, they understand that effort makes them stronger. Therefore, they put in extra time and effort, and that leads to higher achievement. They have a *growth mindset*. But the opposite is true, too—when we believe we can't do something, we might not even try.[31] That's a *fixed mindset*, and it's dangerous to hindering achievement of one's goals.

---

[31]."Dr. Dweck's Research into Growth Mindset Changed Education Forever," MindsetWorks, https://www.mindsetworks.com/science/.

Recent advances in neuroscience have shown us that we can increase our neural growth by the actions we take, such as using good strategies, asking questions, practicing, and following good habits.[32]

Now, a general rule of thumb is that it takes a minimum of twenty-one days to replace a bad habit with a good one. However old you are, or wherever you are in your journey to positive thinking, it's not going to happen overnight. You've been doing things a certain way for a long time. So go easy on yourself. Give yourself time to make lasting changes, and celebrate small victories along the way.

Welcome the Wisdom You Gain by Making Mistakes

We also grow by making mistakes! Think about it—haven't you learned a lot more from your mistakes than you have from your successes?

Making mistakes is so important to the growth of our brains, in fact, that some scientists believe we should not tell our children they are smart. If we tell them they're smart and then they make a mistake—which they will, eventually—they will think, "Oh, no! I'm not smart after all!" Then they'll be reluctant to challenge themselves again, for fear of making another mistake.

Jo Boaler, PhD, is The Nomellini–Olivier Professor of Mathematics Education at the Stanford University Graduate School of Education. She says that when people perform well (academically or otherwise) at early ages and are labeled smart or gifted, they become less likely to challenge themselves. They become less likely to make

---
32. Ibid.

mistakes because they stay in their comfortable comfort zone and stop growing. And that fixed mindset persists through adulthood. Boaler says, "It's imperative that we don't praise kids by telling them they're smart. You can tell kids that they've done something fantastic, but don't label them as smart."[33]

Along these same lines, it can be detrimental to your kids' development if you compare them. Don't say, "This is my athletic one, and this is my creative one." This could cause your "athletic" kid to think he isn't creative, and It could cause your "creative" kid to think she isn't athletic.

This kind of wisdom is critical for us to know as parents, leaders, teachers, coaches, and mentors. I know from firsthand experience that negative thoughts start inundating us as early as childhood. As adults, we can stop the cycle of self-critical kids growing up to be self-critical adults, simply by being aware of the impact our words and actions have on kids.

As a parent of two children myself, it has been challenging for me to find different ways to praise them that don't fall into the "fixed mindset" narrative. Here are some examples that have been helpful for me to use:

---

33. James Hamblin, "100 Percent Is Overrated," *The Atlantic*, June 30, 2015, https://www.theatlantic.com/education/archive/2015/06/the-s-word/397205/.

Fixed Mindset	Growth Mindset
"You are really smart."	"You worked really hard to attain a great grade."
"Science just isn't your subject."	"It looks like you don't understand this yet. Let's see what strategies we can try to help you improve."
"You're a natural."	"It looks like that was easy for you. Let's try something more challenging."

Dr. Bruce Lipton: We Can Change Our Bodies by Retraining Our Thinking

Like all the other concepts in this book, the idea of retraining our thinking—building mental toughness—is based on science.

For example, Bruce H. Lipton, PhD, is a former medical school professor and research scientist. In his best-selling book *The Biology of Belief*, he examines in great detail the mechanisms by which cells receive and process information.

Dr. Lipton concludes that genes and DNA do not control our biology; rather, DNA is controlled by signals coming from *outside* the cells, including the energetic messages emanating from our positive and negative thoughts. His research indicates that our bodies can change physically as we retrain our thinking.

He says, "Your beliefs act like filters on a camera, changing how you see the world. And your biology adapts to those beliefs. When we truly recognize that our beliefs are that powerful, we hold the key to freedom. While we cannot readily change the codes of our genetic blueprints, we can change our minds and, in the process, switch the blueprints used to express our genetic potential."[34]

How a Paraplegic Regained Physical Vitality by Changing How He Thinks

Now, Dr. Lipton's explanation is kind of complex. To boil it down to real life, let's look at an example of how this plays out in real life.

Ken Ware, an Australian trainer, is the mastermind behind a therapy called the "Ware K health trigger process." It involves a patient closing his or her eyes and slowly lifting a small amount of weight. Soon, the patient's body begins shaking violently, almost to the point of convulsing, and the patient is instructed to just let it happen. Ware has experimented with the treatment since 1982. His strategy helped a patient regain use of badly broken legs and go on to win a powerlifting world championship, among other success stories.[35]

A 2013 article in the medical journal *Frontiers in Clinical and Translational Physiology* discussed how this therapy works: by literally shaking the body's nervous system out of a pattern, such as partial paralysis, and

---

34. Bruce H. Lipton, PhD, *The Biology of Belief: Unleashing the Power of Consciousness, Matter, and Miracles* (Carlsbad, California: Hay House, 2005), 137.
35. Reed Tucker, "The Crazy Way This Paraplegic Learned to Walk Again," *New York Post*, March 27, 2016, https://nypost.com/2016/03/27/the-crazy-way-this-paraplegic-learned-to-walk-again/.

forcing it to reorganize in a more orderly fashion.[36]

One person whose life Ware has transformed using this strategy is John Maclean. One day in 1988, he was riding his bike when a nine-ton truck hit him. He suffered head and chest trauma, a broken arm and pelvis, a pulmonary contusion, a broken back, and a partially severed spinal cord. Maclean was rendered an incomplete paraplegic, with no use of his right leg and only 25 percent of the left.[37]

After years of believing he would never walk again, Maclean found out about Ware's treatment and started working with Ware. After just four days in the therapy, lifting the weights with his arms, Maclean's nervous system was reset to the point that he could take his first tenuous steps. Ware said that because Maclean's spinal cord had not been fully severed, impulses were still getting through to his legs, and the inability to control his limbs was partially mental. Ware later took him to a beach, where Maclean attempted to run. He fell on his first two attempts, but on the third he stayed upright.[38]

Talk about mental toughness! Isn't it amazing what can be accomplished simply by changing the way we think? And, going back to the concept of health neuroscience that we discussed earlier, there is a strong correlation between our mental strength and our physical strength.

Another example of mental toughness that amazes me is the story of Dr. Joe Dispenza, an author, speaker, researcher, and chiropractor who is known as a "muscle

---

36. Ibid.
37. Ibid.
38. Ibid.

memory" expert. The reason why he does what he does is because when he was twenty-three, he got hit by an SUV while riding his bicycle in a triathlon. A police officer motioned for him to turn right, and as he did, he was looking at the police officer. He didn't see the oncoming truck. The truck hit him, and six vertebrae in his spine were broken.[39]

Doctors told Dispenza he needed surgery to avoid becoming paralyzed—but he never did. Instead, he healed himself. He says he did two things: "First, every day I would put all of my conscious attention on this intelligence within me and give it a plan, a template, a vision, with very specific orders, and then I would surrender my healing to this greater mind that has unlimited power, allowing it to do the healing for me. And second, I wouldn't let any thought slip by my awareness that I didn't want to experience."[40] He literally rebuilt his spine through visualization!

In fact, a medical breakthrough called "mirror therapy" uses vision to treat the pain that people with amputated limbs sometimes feel in their missing limbs. Mirror therapy does this by tricking the brain: it gives the illusion that the missing limb is moving, as the person looks at the real, remaining limb in a mirror. This way, the brain ignores the fact that it receives no signal of movement from the amputated limb itself. Researchers are learning more about how to use virtual reality to further develop this therapy.[41]

---

39. "How I Healed Myself After Breaking Six Vertebrae," Dr. Joe Dispenza, HealYourLife, May 23, 2014, https://www.healyourlife.com/how-i-healed-myself-after-breaking-6-vertebrae.
40. Ibid.
41. "Fooling the Brain, Fooling the Pain: The Role of Mirror Therapy and Modern Uses in Virtual Reality," Charles Faure, Annabelle Limballe, and Hugo A. Kerhervé, Frontiers in Young Minds, July 3, 2019, https://kids.frontiersin.org/article/10.3389/frym.2019.00091.

Ken Ware and Dr. Joe Dispenza could have easily wallowed in self-pity and given up. But they didn't. Tony Ewing, an entrepreneur focused on behavioral science, says people with mental toughness do not pity themselves. He writes, "For every excuse you create, you clone a mental 'roommate' who constantly nags at you whenever you face the slightest difficulty." He explains, "You're hungry? Your roommate tells you that you *must* eat or you'll die. You're tired? The excuse comes to mind that you can't possibly work any harder. By contrast, mentally strong people rid themselves of this enemy early on." Ewing says we have to be aware when we are pitying ourselves and consciously stop those thoughts.[42]

I think all this science is incredible. We cannot underestimate the power of visualization, which can help us develop mental toughness—the bedrock upon which all the other self-help concepts are built.

Six Practical Ways to Build Mental Toughness

We have to be mentally tough if we're going to be able to fight off the constant barrage of negativity that life, Lucy, and our own brains toss our way. Here are six practical ways I build mental toughness.

---

42. "5 Habits of Mentally Strong People—Based on Science, Tony Ewing, *Forbes*, July 24, 2020, https://www.forbes.com/sites/tonyewing/2020/07/24/5-habits-of-mentally-strong-people-based-on-science/#66310db67a33.

1. Thou Shalt Not Be a Weenie—Kick Fear to the Curb

In a recent conversation with one of my financial advisors, he told me he hadn't made his calls yet. He was supposed to have made them but hadn't gotten to it.

Within one minute, his brain had gone from "I didn't make my calls" to "I'm such a loser" to "My wife is going to leave me because I'm not going to make any money" to "I'm going to be homeless!" He got to "I'm going to be homeless!" in less than one minute. It's a great example of a basic truth of human nature: we tend to be catastrophic thinkers.

Remember the "negativity bias" and "catastrophic thinking" we discussed a bit earlier? This is the way it manifests in our everyday lives. We take the slightest possibility of a negative outcome and blow it way out of proportion.

One way to kick fear to the curb is to face your fears head-on instead of letting them consume you.

Psychologists call this approach "exposure therapy." It's a psychological treatment that was developed to help people confront their fears. When people are fearful of something, they tend to avoid the feared objects, activities, or situations. According to the American Psychological Association, although this avoidance might help reduce feelings of fear in the short term, it can make the fear become even worse over the long term. In such situations, a psychologist often creates a safe environment in which to "expose" individuals to the things they fear and avoid to help reduce fear and decrease avoidance.[43]

I'll give you an example of this in my life. I have always been terrified of spiders. I sometimes have nightmares about spiders crawling on me. It's horrifying. Then, while I'm awake, if I see a spider scurry across the floor at home, I tend to let out a blood-curdling shriek, and my husband knows he needs to come squish a spider. I got tired of being a weenie, so I started doing exposure therapy. First, I worked on getting to the point where I could get close enough to just look at a spider. Before, I couldn't even look at it; I would scream and run away. Then I told myself, "OK, I'm just going to go stare at it." I would stare at a spider sometimes for two minutes and tell myself, "He's not that harmful." Eventually, I got to the point where I could kill it myself. I would tell myself, "I'm going to take this shoe and smash it."

Then I took it a step further. I got to the point where I would say, "OK, I don't really need to kill the spider. What if I could just put it outside?" I got myself to the point where I could put a stick where the spider was, let the spider crawl onto the stick, and throw it outside. Now, if it's a brown recluse spider or a black widow, I'm going to kill it. But I'll let the Daddy Long Legs spiders live. They kill other spiders, so I tell them, "You just keep chilling up there and kill all the other spiders that are in the house."

---

43. "What Is Exposure Therapy?" American Psychological Association, https://www.apa.org/ptsd-guideline/patients-and-families/exposure-therapy.

That was a huge accomplishment for me because of how terrified I used to be of spiders. What are some of the fears you have been avoiding? Think about ways you can expose yourself to them in order to overcome them.

Thou shalt not be a weenie. Kick fear to the curb.

2. Let It Go (Follow the Five-Minute Rule)

Recently, I was having a discussion with a friend, but it was a rather one-sided conversation.

He was telling me a personal, and negative, story—the same story he'd told me at least six times before. He was pissed off about an interaction he'd had with another person in his life and simply couldn't let it go.

I said to him, "How much more time are you going to let this person suck away from you? You've spent so much time and energy ruminating on what happened, but it's done now. I know that was upsetting, but I think it might be helpful for you to move forward and focus on something else."

I get it. In the past, I had a tendency to dwell on things. If something didn't go my way, I would think about it for a *long* time. I always needed to get it off my chest, so I would tell someone—maybe my husband, or a colleague—but then I still wasn't satisfied, so I would tell a second person, and a third. Then I realized I would end up telling five people the same story about how I was wronged.

One day, I heard about the *five-minute rule*. It states that if you can't change something, it's OK to allow yourself to be upset by it—but for five minutes only. Then you have to move on. You're not allowed to waste any more time thinking about it—or in my case, telling *everyone* you know about how upset you are.

The story I heard about when I first learned of the five-minute rule was about a man who had been in an accident and could no longer walk, so he used a wheelchair. Realizing he couldn't change his situation, he decided he had to accept the situation. He knew his reaction to his situation was his choice: he could either be angry about it, or he could become the happiest guy in a wheelchair you've ever seen. In fact, the guy started decorating his wheelchair so he could inspire others who were recently injured, particularly children.

How we will respond to our circumstances is our own personal choice.

Not long ago, I was in Las Vegas for a board meeting. Because I was a nursing mother, when I traveled, I would pre-arrange with my hotel to get into my room early so I could pump breast milk for my baby.

This time was no different. I had made arrangements, and the hotel staff was great. They said, "Yes, of course we can accommodate you. No problem."

I flew to Vegas from my home in California, which is a short flight of about one hour. But when you add the airport security check and the ride to the hotel, it took me a total of five hours to get to my hotel.

When I got there, it was really busy, and my room wasn't ready. It was going to be several hours before they could let me in. I was already past my window of when I needed to pump, so I asked for a private area where I could pump since my room wasn't ready. The hotel staff apologized, saying they didn't have a place to accommodate me. They suggested that I use the public women's bathroom, which had the power outlet I needed.

At first, I was fuming. I had made arrangements—how dare they suggest I go into a public restroom and embarrass myself? *It's so unprofessional they aren't accommodating me, blah blah blah.* But then I remembered the five-minute rule.

Being at this board meeting was important. Feeding my child was important. The hotel didn't have a breastfeeding room, and I didn't have a choice—there was nothing I could change. So instead of being angry, I decided to have fun.

I went into the bathroom they suggested and found the outlet, which was in front of the mirror, right where the entrance is. If you're a mom who has pumped, you know it's not a quick two-minute thing. It typically takes twenty to thirty minutes. I turned on Pandora from my cell phone and started rocking out as I pumped. There was no privacy; women were walking in and out. Rather than allow myself to be mad and embarrassed when women walked in, I chose to be cheerful, and I engaged them. It was kind of amazing because every single woman who walked in praised me and said things like, "I remember those days" or "Good for you! What an amazing mother you are." Some started singing to the music I was playing.

So the situation that had been on the verge of ruining my mood for the day actually turned into a really positive, uplifting event for me because all these women were giving me kudos. If I had let myself be mad and cowered in the corner with a frowny face, it would have been a negative experience.

The five-minute rule has been very powerful for me. It helps me focus my energy and efforts on the things I *can* control and change. I no longer feel sorry for myself; I just change my attitude, and that gives me the mental toughness to change the outcome.

3. Reframe the Way You View Things

There were times in my career when I questioned my decision to enter financial services. Earlier, I told you that's the career advice my guidance counselor in high school had recommended for me because I have always been good at math. So I did, but finance was never my original passion. I wondered if I was in the right career. I wondered if I might be happier doing something else. I remembered how much I loved theatre, and being in financial services is sort of a 180 from theatre.

But then I decided to look at this in a different way. I asked myself what I loved about theatre in school. Was it the scripts I was reading? No. What I loved was performing in front of audiences. I loved inspiring people through art. I decided, "I can do the same thing in financial services!"

So I combined my passion for inspiring people in the world of financial services. As a financial advisor, before I entered management, I was inspiring my clients to take charge of their financial future by getting their finances in order. When I became a manager, I began inspiring my team to be valuable sources of guidance for their clients. Next, I began speaking to audiences to reach more people in these areas.

Today, as I travel around the country doing public speaking, I realize that I *am* inspiring audiences. I don't need to be in theatre to do that. I just needed to reframe my passion in a new way.

The key is to blend what you love to do with what you excel at. I once read an article in which the author suggested the concept of making two things you love "have sex" to create a "baby" that is the combination of those things. For example, if you love both yoga and animals, you can teach goat yoga. (Yes, it's a real thing. Look it up!)

Maybe you are a manager who loves to be active outdoors, and being stuck inside an office is a real downer for you. But you love coaching, mentoring, and leading your team members. Why not reframe the way you conduct your staff reviews? Instead of sitting in your office or in a conference room, ask each staff member if he or she would like to take a walk with you outside while you discuss the review. Chances are, many of your staff members will love the idea and appreciate the change in routine.

Whether you're at home, in the office, doing volunteer work, or doing something else, reframe the way you look at things. Try to view your passions, talents, and career from a different angle.

4. Change Your Response to an Event

I attended a training session recently, and the instructor gave us a great formula, sort of like algebra, only with letters instead of numbers:

$$E \times R = O$$

This stands for:

Event X Response = Outcome

The "E" represents the constant, the thing that isn't going to change. The "R" is the element of the equation that can change. When you "multiply" the two, you get the outcome.

The example the instructor gave us was that 30 percent of people like the rain, and 70 percent don't like the rain—maybe because they can't do things outside or because it messes up their shoes. But we can't change the rain. It's an event we have no control over. The only part of the equation we can change is our *response* to the rain.

So if it rains (event) and you get really annoyed (response), then you're going to have a lousy day (outcome). But if it rains (event) and you change your plans accordingly by having a great family day of board games by the fireplace, or by taking the opportunity to curl up and read that book you've been meaning to get to (response), you will have a much happier day (outcome).

If you want to be happier, you have to change your response to the events you have no control over. This concept ties in nicely with the five-minute rule.

Did you know that an entire branch of psychology was built around this concept? Viktor Frankl, MD, PhD, a Holocaust survivor, is the founder of *logotherapy*. Dr. Frankl, a psychoanalyst, observed people he was in the concentration camps with during World War II. He wondered why some survived, while others did not.

Dr. Frankl's book, *Man's Search for Meaning*, is considered one of the ten most life-changing books in America. It's easy to see why. In the book, Dr. Frankl writes, "We who lived in concentration camps can remember men who walked through the huts comforting others, giving away their last piece of bread. They may have been small in number, but they offer sufficient proof that everything can be taken from a man but one thing: the last of the human freedoms—to choose one's attitude in any given set of circumstances, to choose one's way."[44]

Yes, we can *choose* how we react to a situation. So we might as well choose to handle it well. Getting annoyed isn't going to change anything; it's just going to ruin your day.

Maybe you have a terrible commute, and driving to and from work every day makes you super-grumpy.

If you can't change your commute for one reason or the other, then you have to find a way to love it—or at least tolerate it. If you love your job and your house and don't want to change either one of those variables, then you have to change your response to the commute. Maybe you can join a carpool and meet some interesting people. Listen to audio books. Or call your mom and catch up while you're driving (hands-free for safety, of course). Do something that will allow you to *enjoy* that time.

---

44. Viktor Frankl, *Man's Search for Meaning* (Boston: Beacon Press, 1959, 1962, 1984, 1992, 2006), 65–66.

Simply by changing your response to the commute—by shifting your mindset—you will change your mood and your life. We have to focus on controlling our negative thoughts. We have to box that bitch who wants us to be miserable.

Dr. Joe Dispenza, the chiropractor I mentioned earlier, talks a lot about "muscle memory" and how we can retrain our minds to get out of negative mode. He combines the fields of quantum physics, neuroscience, brain chemistry, biology, and genetics to show what is truly possible.

In his book *Breaking the Habit of Being Yourself: How to Lose Your Mind and Create a New One*, he says the reason why past efforts to make any lasting change in your life have fallen short "has more to do with your beliefs about why your life is the way it is than with anything else, including a perceived lack of will, time, courage, or imagination. Always, in order to change, we have to come to a new understanding of self and the world so that we can embrace new knowledge and have new experiences. Your past shortfalls can be traced, at their root, to one major oversight: you haven't committed yourself to living by the truth that *your thoughts have consequences so great that they create your reality.*"[45]

Wow! That's powerful. And it's true.

It's all about attitude. We can choose to focus on the negative thoughts that bombard us constantly, or we can choose to focus on positive thoughts instead. Focusing on something gives it fuel, and it becomes even more

---

45. Joe Dispenza, *Breaking the Habit of Being Yourself: How to Lose Your Mind and Create a New One* (Carlsbad, California: Hay House Publishers, 2012,) 4.

prominent in our minds. So we must be intentional about focusing on the positive aspects of any situation.

My business coach gave me some great advice in this area. We all have negative thoughts, so we shouldn't beat ourselves up for having them. We need to simply acknowledge them for what they are and then *redirect* those thoughts and move on. Don't get angry with yourself for having these thoughts. When you do that, you're giving the negative thoughts more fuel.

5. Play to Win, Not to Keep from Losing

High-stakes gamblers play to *win*; they don't play to *avoid losing*. When we play to win, we are calling on our confidence to come out on top. But when we constantly fear failure, we are focused on the negative possibility that we could lose if we overplay our hand.

Have you seen the movie *Crazy Rich Asians*? There is a great scene at the beginning of the movie in which the character played by Constance Wu is teaching her economics class. She is playing a game of poker with a student. She has a losing hand, but she bluffs and beats her student. Then she proceeds to explain to the class that the reason she was able to do so is because the student was "playing not to lose" instead of "playing to win."

I had to stop and ask myself, "Am I playing to win, or am I playing not to lose? Have I been playing it safe because of a fear of failure? Have I not been taking all the shots I should be taking?"

How many times have we not taken that shot because we were afraid of failure? How many times did we not call that prospect, not ask for the bigger sale, not ask that hottie for a date, not ask for the raise or promotion, all because we were afraid to lose? I challenge you to *play to win*!

When Tom Brady was quarterback for the New England Patriots, he played in nine Super Bowls and won six—the most of any football player in NFL history. He knows a thing or two about playing to win. He says, "I think that at the start of a game, you're always playing to win, and then maybe if you're ahead late in the game, you start playing not to lose. The true competitors, though, are the ones who always play to win."

6. Focus on Gratitude

When we are constantly aware of all the wonderful things we have in our lives, that contributes to positive thinking. The lovely actress Doris Day said, "Gratitude is riches. Complaint is poverty."

One reason negativity creeps into our minds is because we compare what we have to what others have. This isn't helpful to anyone. There will always be someone who has something more—more money, a bigger house, a faster sports car, etc. Once you fill your life with all the things you need, want, and love, there's no reason to compare yourself to anyone else. Simply express gratitude for what you do have.

Science shows that a mindset of gratitude can improve our well-being. Glenn Fox, PhD, is the head of program design, strategy, and outreach at USC Performance Science Institute. He explains how this occurs: "The regions associated with gratitude are part of the neural networks that light up when we socialize and experience pleasure," he says. "These regions are also heavily connected to the parts of the brain that control basic emotion regulation, such as heart rate and arousal levels, and are associated with stress relief and thus pain reduction." Other studies show that gratitude increases willpower, helps keep you calm, and can even boost employee morale.[46]

The delightful Anne Frank, wise beyond her young years, once said, "Dead people receive more flowers than living ones because regret is stronger than gratitude." What a wonderful reminder to express gratitude every chance we get, to those who are still living!

Mental toughness is something you can build up every day. And it requires a positive attitude. Whatever you call that little gremlin jerk in your head, you have to control it. You have to box that bitch. If you don't, the fear may consume you, and you risk plodding through life afraid of everything. Lucy and her kind keep us from achieving our potential. It's up to us to change that.

---

46. "What Can the Brain Reveal About Gratitude?" Glenn Fox, *Greater Good Magazine*, Berkeley, August 4, 2017, https://greatergood.berkeley.edu/article/item/what_can_the_brain_reveal_about_gratitude.

John Assaraf: Our Minds Are Keeping Us from Achieving Our Potential

Another expert on the powerful mind–body connection is John Assaraf, founder and CEO of a company called NeuroGym. This program uses neuroscience-based training programs to help individuals and corporations maximize their fullest potential.[47] Just like we work out to keep our bodies in shape, we need to work out our minds to strengthen our mental toughness muscle.

Assaraf coined the term *innercise* to refer to science-based mental and emotional techniques to strengthen your mindset and unleash the hidden power of your brain. Here is what Assaraf says about how our negative habits, thoughts, and emotions hold us back from optimizing our potential: "Lack of knowledge or skill is not what really holds you back. It's your mindset, emotional blocks, and deeply ingrained habits that you must release to clear the path to your greatest victories and successes."[48]

He also says our limiting beliefs, stories, and excuses are "nothing more than reinforced subconscious patterns that cause you to think, feel, and consistently behave in ways that produce the same results over and over again."[49]

I know from personal experience that all these experts on the mind–body connection are right. It's so important to detox our brains so we can replace negative thoughts with positive ones and to replace doubt and fear with hope and confidence.

---

47. Assaraf's NeuroGym website is at https://www.myneurogym.com/.
48. John Assaraf, *Innercise: The New Science to Unlock Your Brain's Hidden Power* (Cardiff, California: Waterside Press, 2018), 1.
49. Ibid.

It's up to each one of us to choose the positive every day, in every situation. You'll get happier and happier as you continue to choose a positive attitude—whatever the circumstances are.

Mind Hacking: Rewrite Your Mental Code

You may have heard the term *mind hacking*. Just like computer hacking, it carries the meaning of reprogramming. We can rewrite the code up there and give ourselves a mental upgrade.

This is the nerdy, scientific part of my book. I want to explain the science behind the concept of changing the way you think.

The brain is an organ in the body, and the mind influences the brain. The subconscious part of our brains regulates most of our thought processes, and we don't even realize it's happening.

To demonstrate this point, I love telling the story about the ant and the owl.

An ant is talking to an owl and says, "Hey, I want to go to the beach. Can you tell me how to get there?"

The owl says, "Yes. Just head straight south, and you'll get there."

The ant starts walking south. He walks for a long, long time but doesn't see the beach. A few days later, he sees the owl again. He says, "Owl, you told me the beach is south.

I've been walking south for days. I'm not at the beach yet. What the heck?"

The owl says, "Yeah, you are going south, but what you don't recognize is that you live on an elephant's back, and the elephant is headed due north."

That's like our subconscious brain versus our conscious brain. Our conscious brain is the ant. We say, "I want to go to the beach," but our subconscious mind, the elephant, is significantly larger and more powerful than our conscious mind. Whatever direction our subconscious mind is headed, that's where we are going.

We can read all the self-help books we want and consciously try to make good decisions about things, but if we don't hack into that subconscious mind that is *way* more powerful and bigger than our conscious mind, then we're not going to make progress the way we want.

Let's say you want to lose weight. For years, you've fantasized about being fit and slender. But ever since you were a kid, you can remember your aunts saying, "Our family just isn't built that way." Or maybe your parents gave you food to comfort you when you were a kid.

Or maybe you want a promotion at work, but you would never go for it because subconsciously, you don't think you're smart enough. Maybe this stems from the fact that your dad always told you, when you were growing up, that you are the "pretty one," and your sister is the "smart one."

Sometimes, we don't even know what the subconscious thoughts are that are holding us back.

But here's the good news: we can replace these deeply embedded thoughts with new thoughts. We just have to tap into the powerful, mysterious brain waves that are already working on our behalf 24/7.

Leverage the Power of Brain Waves

Disclaimer: I am by no means a neuroscientist. However, this kind of shit *fascinates* me, so I study it *ad nauseum*. Let me share what I've learned from professionals in the field because I think you'll find it fascinating, too.

Brain waves are divided into five different bandwidths that scientists believe create a spectrum of human consciousness. Throughout the day and night, our brain waves are part of a feedback loop that is influenced by what we're doing, thinking, and feeling at any given time, or while we sleep.

Here is a description of the five brain-wave bandwidths:[50]

- **Delta waves** (.5 to 3 Hz) are the slowest brain waves. They occur mainly during our deepest state of dreamless sleep.
- **Theta waves** (3 to 8 Hz) occur while we're sleeping, but researchers have also observed them in the deepest states of Zen meditation.

---

50. "Alpha Brain Waves Boost Creativity and Reduce Depression," Christopher Bergland, *Psychology Today*, April 17, 2015, https://www.psychologytoday.com/us/blog/the-athletes-way/201504/alpha-brain-waves-boost-creativity-and-reduce-depression.

- **Alpha waves** (8 to 12 Hz) are present when your brain is in an idling default-state. This typically happens when you are daydreaming or consciously practicing mindfulness or meditation. Alpha waves can also be created by doing aerobic exercise. You are typically in alpha in the first few minutes of waking up or prior to falling asleep.

- **Beta waves** (12-30 Hz) typically dominate our normal waking states of consciousness. They occur when our attention is directed toward cognitive tasks. Beta is considered a "fast" wave activity that is present when we are alert, attentive, focused, and engaged in problem solving or decision making. Depression and anxiety have also been linked to beta waves because they can lead to "rut-like" thinking patterns.

- **Gamma waves** (25 to 100 Hz) typically hover around 40 Hz and are the fastest of the brain-wave bandwidths. Gamma waves relate to simultaneous processing of information from different areas of the brain. They have been associated with higher states of conscious perception.

Alpha waves are the gateway to the unconscious mind—the part that's significantly more powerful than the conscious mind. To mind-hack, to tap into that unconscious mind and reprogram it, we access the mind through our alpha state. Controlling the thoughts and images that you have during *alpha* is incredibly important because those will embed in your subconscious mind. That's why I watch my Mind Movies first thing in the morning—I want to put that positivity and those goals into my mind while I'm still in alpha. It's also why I don't check my email first thing, or read the news right away (which is most often focused on something terrible going on in the world). Those aren't messages I need to send to my subconscious brain.

The Subconscious Mind Rules

In his book *Breaking the Habit of Being Yourself: How to Lose Your Mind and Create a New One,* Dr. Joe Dispenza talks about how accessing the brain through slower waves enables you to "get beyond the analytical mind and enter into the subconscious mind, so you can make real and permanent changes."[51]

Amazingly, only 5 percent of the human mind is governed by the conscious part of the brain, and the other 95 percent is subconscious! So when you are trying to use your conscious brain over your subconscious brain, it's like a snail going up against a rhinoceros.

"When we move into slower brain-wave states," Dispenza writes, "we move deeper into the inner world of the subconscious mind." The slowest wave state that is still awake is about 8 hertz—the low end of alpha. When we can

---

51. Joe Dispenza and Daniel G. Amen, *Breaking the Habit of Being Yourself: How to Lose Your Mind and Create a New One* (Carlsbad, California: Hay House, 2013).

access that frequency, we "enter the operating system of the subconscious, where all of those unwanted habits and behaviors reside, and change them to more productive modes to support us in our lives."[52]

Your subconscious brain is one million times more powerful than your conscious brain. Yes, one million times! That's why we must control our thoughts. A lot goes on in our brains that we aren't even aware of. So we need to be constantly vigilant about tapping into the power of positive thinking. We need to be incredibly protective of our subconscious mind and guard it against negativity.

I used to be a horror-flick junkie. The more zombie guts and blood, the more interested I was in watching the movie. I loved the "thrill" of being scared. I had nightmares often, mostly about zombies, but that still didn't detract me from binge-watching *The Walking Dead*. As I started to learn more about the brain, I became more curious about the impact that my horror addiction may have been having on my mental health. The results of my research were enough for me to decide to stop watching horror films.

The reason why horror movies are so effective at "scaring" you is that at a subconscious level, your brain thinks what is happening in the movie is happening to you. So if you are watching *Friday the 13th*, your brain

---

52. Ibid., 24.

thinks Jason with his terrifying hockey mask is standing right outside your door, coming to get you. Scary movies bypass the conscious part of your brain (which knows Jason is totally fabricated) to tap directly into the fight or flight response (which thinks he is as real as your spouse sitting next to you).

The amygdala is the part of your brain that has evolved to respond immediately to anything that looks like a threat, regardless of how real it actually is. Once the amygdala sounds the alarm to your body, your hypothalamus tells your adrenal glands to inject you with a giant boost of adrenaline. That's why your heart starts beating faster and faster, just in case you need to be prepared to run away from Jason when he breaks through your front door.

The brain is so powerful that a fictional character on a screen can cause a physical response from your body. There have been cases of horror movies causing stress, anxiety, and insomnia.

Unsurprisingly, my zombie dreams completely disappeared a couple of months after I stopped watching horror movies.

I shared earlier about my fear of spiders. I also used to suffer from incredibly real spider dreams. When I was nineteen, I started having dreams of thousands of spiders overtaking my bed, to the point I would stand on my bed, stomping all over it, screaming, trying to kill the spiders (a couple of roommates and my poor husband have unfortunately been awoken in the middle of the night with that ridiculous scene). My spider dreams also stopped once I stopped watching horror films. Even if your brain doesn't translate scary movies into dramatic dreams like mine did for me, I encourage you to take a sabbatical from negativity and see if you notice any differences.

Perhaps for thirty days, stay away from scary movies, negative news, and social media posts. Trade those for uplifting stories, inspiration, or creative activities. You might be surprised at how much better you feel by this simple act.

Eliminating the negative is one aspect, but replacing it with positive is where the magic really happens. I read at least one positive quote every single day. With Pinterest, Instagram, and podcasts galore, there is no shortage of places to find positive messaging. Find sites and people you connect with, and get your fill of positivity. I encourage you to have an accountability partner around this. Work with someone who is likeminded and wants to live his or her best life. I have many of those people in my tribe already, but I also have a few additional go-to people. When we see something inspirational, we share it with each other. And we call each other out on things when one of us starts going down a negative rabbit hole.

I want to be very clear that not all my bad habits changed overnight. It's not like one day I just completely transformed everything in my world. This has been a journey, slowly figuring out what works for me. As I have fine-tuned the way I do things over the years, it has helped me incorporate some of this brain science to know how to make it stick.

I want to end this chapter on a super-positive and fun note. One of my favorite YouTube videos is of an adorable six-year-old girl named Jessica, who is standing on the bathroom vanity, shouting positive affirmations to herself in the mirror, with great gusto. In the past ten years, this video has been viewed more than twenty million times. The video is less than one minute long, but I think it will really make your day. It's titled "Jessica's 'Daily Affirmation,'" and it's at https://www.youtube.com/watch?v=qR3rK0kZFkg.

Isn't it fascinating that we are so divinely equipped to achieve amazing accomplishments?

CHAPTER 4

Deliberate Creation: Prioritize Your Time

> "Nobody's life is ever all balanced. It's a conscious decision to choose your priorities every day."
>
> —Elisabeth Hasselbeck, Retired American Television Personality

Good things come to those who wait. Great things come to those who take action. We talked about goal setting in chapter 2. You can do goal *setting* with a pencil, but goal *getting* needs to be done with your legs. You have to take action! When you are actively managing your time, you can be deliberate about creating awesome things.

Look, we all feel like there's never enough time in a day. Everyone feels that way—Oprah, the president, Olympic athletes, CEOs of major companies, and celebrities. The reality is that we all have the same amount of time every day to make things happen—24 hours, 1,440 minutes, 86,400 seconds. None of the ultra-successful people in the world have figured out how to *expand* time. They've learned how to *prioritize* it.

Watch Out for the Time Vampires

Time is our most valuable resource. We can't save it in a bank. We can't take out a time loan. We can't invest it and hope for a return of more time. Once that precious commodity is gone, it's gone. That's why we have to prioritize what's most important to us. That's why we need to keep our vision front of mind all the time and spend our time on those activities that will bring our vision into reality.

The first step is to really inspect where you're spending your time. Years ago, a coach of mine asked me to track my time every thirty minutes for two weeks straight. I was shocked to find out how much time I was wasting. Too much TV, too many "You got a minute?" interruptions at work, too much time on boring household chores. It was a tedious exercise, but incredibly eye-opening. I've done this exercise many times since the original assignment, and each time, I've figured out how to regain at least four hours per week of unproductive time. If you regain four hours per week, you will regain an additional *five work weeks* per year. Can you imagine the possibilities of recapturing five weeks?

There's time for that vacation after all. Time to learn that language you've been wanting to learn or to practice that golf swing you've been trying to perfect.

According to the 2018 American Time Use Survey (ATUS) conducted by the US Bureau of Labor Statistics, on an average day, nearly everyone age 15 and over (96 percent) engaged in some sort of leisure activity, such as watching TV, socializing, or exercising. Men spent 5.7 hours per day in these activities, compared with 4.9 hours for women. Watching TV was the leisure activity that occupied the most time (2.8 hours per day), accounting for just over half of all leisure time, on average.

Wow, 2.8 hours per day is a lot! If you watch TV for 2.8 hours per day, that's 19.6 hours per week, 84 hours per month, and 1,022 hours per year! Imagine what you could accomplish if you cut back just on watching TV.

But TV isn't even the worst time thief anymore! A 2019 study by EMarketer, Inc., reports that in 2019, for the first time ever, Americans spent more time staring down at their phones and tablets than they do watching television. The average US adult spends 3 hours and 43 minutes on mobile devices. About 70 percent of their time is spent on their smartphones, alone.

Have you ever monitored how much time you spend watching TV, watching videos on your phone, or hanging out on social media? It might surprise you. The next time you find yourself saying you "don't have time" to do something important, take a look at where you are spending your time!

Once you realize where you're being inefficient with your time, you can take positive steps toward filling your valuable, finite time with more meaningful activities. One great tool that can help you do that is a planner.

Keep a Planner

Get a good planner, and keep it with you all the time. It will help you prioritize your time and activities.

I swear by the Panda Planner because of its helpful guided sections that ask questions about what I'm going to do to make the coming week great. Its weekly planner is what I use during my Power Hour (which we will discuss in chapter 5), and every morning, before I start my day, I fill out the daily planner.

It gives me space to write down my gratitude list and affirmations, my daily schedule, my six highest priorities for the day, and tasks I need to get done. I still keep an electronic calendar, but taking a couple of minutes in the morning to think through my day and write with my hand helps me feel really organized and ready to conquer the day.

There is also a reflection section in this planner. I take a few minutes at the end of each day to reflect on how the day went and what I need to do differently if it didn't go as I hoped.

The man who created the Panda Planner, Michael Leip, has an inspiring story. He created this planner to get himself organized and feeling positive when he was overwhelmed by the symptoms of Lyme disease, traumatic brain injury, and cancer. He turned to proven research in positive psychology and neuroscience and created this system to get his life back on track.[53]

You might already use a digital calendar of some kind—on your phone, your Apple Watch, your laptop. But taking a few minutes in the morning to think through the day ahead and tangibly *write* in a planner helps solidify your plan and conquer your day.

Prioritizing Your Own Time Will Inspire Others

As leaders, one of our greatest responsibilities is to live up to our fullest potential in every aspect of our lives. Doing that will empower and give permission to others to do the same. We are role models for our kids, for our clients, and for our teams.

I've shared the strategies in this chapter with the teams I lead at work. One of the most rewarding things

---

53. Panda Planner, https://pandaplanner.com/.

for me is seeing the positive impact those practices have made in their lives.

What are we really doing with our 168 hours each week? That's a lot of time! Like we talked about earlier, we tend to waste that time. We waste it watching TV, scrolling through our Facebook feeds, or dwelling on negative thoughts. These are traps any of us can fall into. But when we start to get our time back, we realize there's plenty of time to do all the things we want to do. We need to prioritize the important activities and stop doing the shit we don't want to do.

That window of 168 hours per week is *your* time. Invest it in *you*.

Don't Wait for a Near-Death Experience to Appreciate Time

Again, time is our most valuable resource. Planning and prioritizing our time will help us make sure we spend our precious time doing the things that will help us achieve our vision. It's sad that some people don't figure this out until they have a near-death experience.

After author Olessia Kantor's plane crash-landed in the depths of the African jungle—and she survived—she says she learned that time is of the absolute essence. "Normally, we take our time when approaching a task, rushing in the final moments to accomplish it, and fearful we might fail in the face of a looming deadline. Understanding urgency has changed my life. I no longer postpone anything that is important to me."[54]

Leadership coach and author Angela Kambouris was close to death due to complications from pneumonia. Here's what she said she learned from that experience: "Life changes within seconds. Decisions are made in a moment. Understanding urgency is a game changer. Don't postpone anything that is important to you. Express your love for things and for people with greater frequency, and maximize every opportunity to appreciate those around you."[55]

Don't wait for a near-death experience to appreciate how precious your time is. Be incredibly selective about how you spend your time. Get off boards you don't want to serve on, take more vacations with your family, and stop doing things that don't totally inspire you. In your business, stop doing things that aren't revenue-producing for you. Don't let the time vampires and "fires" suck precious hours away from you, your vision, your family, and your business.

Be constantly aware of how precious time is. Make the most of your time by nurturing positive experiences and relationships. One of the best ways to get control of your time, in my opinion, is to establish a routine, which we'll discuss next.

---

54. Olessia Kantor, "Live Without Regrets: Lessons from a Near-Death Experience," Tiny Buddha, February 2, 2016, https://tinybuddha.com/blog/live-without-regrets-lessons-from-a-near-death-experience/.
55. Angela Kambouris, "7 Life Lessons from a Near-Death Experience," Thrive Global, September 20, 2017, https://thriveglobal.com/stories/7-life-lessons-from-a-near-death-experience/.

CHAPTER 5

Adopt a Routine to Stay Positive

> "You will never change your life until you change something you do daily. The secret of your success is found in your daily routine."
>
> —John C. Maxwell

I have discovered two secret weapons against Lucy, naysayers, caca, and negative thoughts: my Miracle Mornings, which is how I begin each day, and my Weekly Power Hour, which is how I end each week. By building these times for intentional planning and reflection into my schedule, I am able to handle the craziness of life in a much calmer way.

Now, you might already have a routine you're happy with. But does your routine reinforce your goals and vision? Does it keep you positive? Please just hear me out, and perhaps there are elements from this routine you can adopt into your own.

Miracle Mornings—A Positive Way to Begin Each Day

I discovered my first powerfully productive strategy in one of my favorite books, *The Miracle Morning* by Hal Elrod. He says you should always start your morning by taking care of yourself and getting into the right mental state before tackling your day.

When I started following the morning routine he suggests, it was like a magic elixir that helped me fend off the negative thoughts that had held me back all my life. I wouldn't start a day without it now!

Elrod calls his suggested routine "Life SAVERS,"[56] and here's what the acronym stands for:

---

56. Hal Elrod, *The Miracle Morning: The Not-So-Obvious Secret Guaranteed to Transform Your Life* (Before 8AM) (Hal Elrod International, Inc., 2012).

- **S**ilence
- **A**ffirmations
- **V**isualization
- **E**xercise
- **R**eading
- **S**cribing

The Six Powerful Elements of My Miracle Mornings

I strongly recommend beginning each day with this routine. Next, I'll explain what each letter in "SAVERS" represents, how to use each activity during your morning routine, and a little bit of science behind the importance of each activity.

S Is for *Silence*

Silence is...exactly what it says it is. Simply sit (or lie down, or stand) in silence and breathe, and let this quiet time clear your mind and calm your inner being. Yes, we're talking about something like meditation, and I know that at first, this will be *impossible* for some people. If you're anything like I was when I first started this routine, the mere thought of meditatively sitting in silence was torture. My mind is too busy, always go-go-go.

Try it. Allow yourself to just *be*. Relax your brain. Start with just one minute, and eventually, you'll come to love your silent moments with yourself. I promise.

Two apps I really like for calming my mind are Calm and Headspace:

1. **Calm** (https://www.calm.com/) features unique audio content that strengthens mental fitness and tackles some of the biggest mental health challenges of today: stress, anxiety, insomnia, and depression. The most popular feature on Calm is a ten-minute meditation called "The Daily Calm" that explores a new mindful theme and inspiring concept each day. Calm also contains more than 120 "Sleep Stories" (bedtime stories for grownups), plus sleep music, meditation lessons, nature sounds, videos, multi-day programs, and Calm Masterclasses delivered by world experts.

2. **Headspace** (https://www.headspace.com/about-us) was launched in 2010 by Andy Puddicombe, a meditation and mindfulness expert. He left college to become a monk and traveled the world for ten years. On his website, you can experience the benefits of meditation with guided meditations, animations, articles, and videos.

If you've never tried meditation, these two apps are a fun, easy way to get started.

What Science Says about the Benefits of Silence

Engaging in silence—drowning out the noise pollution— can actually build new cells in our brains! A 2013 study found that two hours of silence can create new cells in the hippocampus region, an area of the brain that's linked to learning, remembering, and emotions.[57]

Being silent can also lower blood pressure, which can help prevent a heart attack; boost the body's immune system; prevent plaque formation in arteries; promote good hormone regulation and the interaction of bodily hormone-related systems; and decrease stress by lowering blood cortisol levels and adrenaline. Just *two minutes* of silence relieves tension in the body and brain and is more relaxing than listening to music, according to a 2006 study published in the journal *Heart*.[58]

A Is for *Affirmations*

Affirmations are basically nice things you say about yourself *to* yourself. Affirmations are statements that something is true—not that you want something to be true, or that you wish for something to be true, but that it *is* true. Here are just a few of thousands of examples:

- "Every action I take works toward my goals."
- "I'm in control of my feelings and desires."
- "Compassion floods my heart and rids me of my anger."
- "I've got this."

---

57. Imke Kirste and Golo Kronenberg, "Is Silence Golden? Effects of Auditory Stimuli on Adult Hippocampal Neurogenesis," ResearchGate, December 2013, https://www.researchgate.net/publication/259110014_Is_silence_golden_Effects_of_auditory_stimuli_and_their_absence_on_adult_hippocampal_neurogenesis.
58. Suzanne Kane, "The Hidden Benefits of Silence," PsychCentral blog, last updated July 8, 2018, https://psychcentral.com/blog/the-hidden-benefits-of-silence/.

- "I breathe in calmness and breathe out anxiety."
- "Money comes to me easily and effortlessly."
- "I attract abundance."
- "I am too big a gift to this world to feel self-pity."
- "I love and approve of myself."
- "I trust myself."
- "The answer is right before me, even if I am not seeing it yet."
- "The past has no power over me anymore."
- "I give up the habit of criticizing myself."
- "I am filled with peace and serenity."

Some people say affirmations out loud; I prefer to say them in my head. I tailor my affirmations to what is front of mind for me at the time.

What Science Says about the Benefits of Affirmations

Like many of the other experts we have talked about, Walter E. Jacobson, MD, believes there is value in affirmations. He says our subconscious mind plays a major role in the actualization of our lives and the manifestation of our desires. What we believe about ourselves at a subconscious level can have a significant impact on the outcome of events.[59]

---

59. Kathryn J. Lively, PhD, "Affirmations: The Why, What, How, and What If?" *Psychology Today*, March 12, 2014, https://www.psychologytoday.com/us/blog/smart-relationships/201403/affirmations-the-why-what-how-and-what-if.

When we repeat affirmations—positive statements—to ourselves, it causes us to focus on positive outcomes. They lead us to believe great things about ourselves. And when we believe these things, even subconsciously, we're more likely to achieve positive outcomes.

A team of researchers at Carnegie Mellon conducted a study to find out how beneficial self-affirmations are to people's well-being. They found that affirmations actually buffer stress and improve problem-solving performance in underperforming and chronically stressed individuals.[60]

V Is for *Visualization*

We talked a lot about visualization already, but let's dive in a little deeper here. Visualization simply means creating visual images of your dreams and goals in your mind. Close your eyes, or, if you've created a vision board, look at it and visualize, or picture, yourself achieving all those dreams.

Either in your mind's eye or in a physical representation, zero in on your goals. Imagine what it will look and feel like once you reach them. You can visualize the day ahead of you going perfectly—enjoying your work, laughing with your spouse, and easily accomplishing all you intend to. Elite athletes do this all the time—they visualize the win. It's a way to program your brain for ultimate motivation.

Here's an exercise to help you visualize yourself already succeeding.

---

60. J. David Creswell, et al., "Self-Affirmation Improves Problem-Solving under Stress," PLOS ONE, May 1, 2013, https://journals.plos.org/plosone/article?id=10.1371/journal.pone.0062593.

Begin by establishing a highly specific goal, perhaps one of the ones you crafted in chapter 2. Imagine the future; you have already achieved your goal. Hold a mental "picture" of it as if it were occurring to you right at that moment. Imagine the scene in as much detail as possible. Engage as many of the five senses as you can in your visualization. Who are you with? Which emotions are you feeling right now? What are you wearing? Is there a smell in the air? What do you hear? What is your environment like? Sit with a straight spine when you do this. Practice at night or in the morning (just before or after sleep). Eliminate any doubts that come to you. Repeat this practice often.

What Science Says about the Benefits of Visualization

Did you know that your brain cannot distinguish between a memory that really happened and one that you made up?[61]

This is great news! It means that we can trick our brains into making something that is unknown *known*. In this way, visualization can help us overcome fear and anxiety, which originate because we are uneasy about the unknown.

In an *Entrepreneur* article, Emilie Pelletier writes, "When you imagine something vividly and with emotion, your brain chemistry changes as though the experience was real, and your mind records it as a real memory... Because of this characteristic of the mind, we can use visualization to overcome fear and build self-confidence,

---

61. Daniel L. Schacter, et al., "The Future of Memory: Remembering, Imagining, and the Brain," US National Library of Medicine, November 21, 2012, https://www.ncbi.nlm.nih.gov/pmc/articles/PMC3815616/.

by 'making the unknown known.' It can also help you achieve your goals. If you can vividly imagine and visualize a future situation, your mind will record it as a real memory. The situation will become something known, something you've 'already experienced.'"[62]

The human brain is an incredible and complex mechanism. Whatever we focus on actually determines our perception of reality. The biological explanation behind this phenomenon is called the *reticular activating system*, or RAS. It's a network of neurons located in the brain that make sure our brains don't have to deal with more information than we can handle. The RAS serves as a filter. Out of all the information coming to our senses from the environment, it selects what the conscious mind will notice and give attention to. Without our RAS, our brains would be overwhelmed with data.[63]

The RAS notices what it believes is important. It prioritizes everything that concerns our survival and safety, as well as the things that match the current content of our minds: beliefs, thoughts, emotions, etc. Your RAS constantly looks for information in your environment that matches and reinforces your thoughts and belief systems. It is the mechanism that is at work when you purchase a particular vehicle and then, all of a sudden, you see that vehicle everywhere you go—on the freeway, in every shopping-center parking lot, etc.

Author Pelletier says in the *Entrepreneur* article,

---

62. Emilie Pelletier, "4 Scientific Reasons Why Visualization Will Increase Your Chances to Succeed," *Entrepreneur*, January 24, 2018, https://entrepreneurs.maqtoob.com/4-scientific-reasons-why-visualization-will-increase-your-chances-to-succeed-5515ef2dbdb7.
63. Ibid.

"Your RAS is like your inner GPS. If you want your GPS to work to your advantage—at noticing opportunities that will take you closer to your objectives—you must program it accordingly. And the best way to program it is by visualizing your goals."[64]

In order to leverage our brain power for optimum advantage, we need to practice keeping our goals front and center. Take note of visual cues that align with your goals. For example, if you see a lake house in a magazine, and you've been dreaming about a lake house like that, tear out that photo and tack it to your vision board. Awareness is the key. Constantly be aware of your vision, and look for examples of that vision manifesting in your life.

E Is for *Exercise*

Of course exercise is vital to your physical and emotional well-being, but you don't have to run a 5K every morning before work. (Most of us don't have the time or desire for that.) But get some form of exercise in, even if you don't have time for a full workout. Just pumping out sixty seconds of jumping jacks will elevate your heart rate, energize you, and help you wake up. (I always need help waking up. I am *not* a morning person!)

When you exercise in the morning, it increases your ability to be alert and focused throughout your day and gives you a lasting boost of energy.

---

64. Ibid.

What Science Says about the Benefits of Exercise

We all know how exercise benefits our bodies, but it gives our mental and emotional health a huge boost, too.

According to Sarah Gingell, PhD, a psychologist and counselor, exercise is well known to stimulate the body to produce endorphins and enkephalins, the body's natural feel-good hormones that can make problems seem more manageable. She says, "The simple act of focusing on exercise can give us a break from current concerns and damaging self-talk. Further, depending on the activity, people may benefit from calming exercises, be energized, and get outside or interact with others, all of which are known to improve mood and general health."[65]

You might be wondering just how much exercise it takes to benefit your emotional well-being.

Madhukar Trivedi, MD, a psychiatrist, found that three or more sessions per week of aerobic exercise or resistance training, for forty-five to sixty minutes per session, can help treat even chronic depression. He says effects tend to be noticed after about four weeks (which is how long neurogenesis takes), and training should be continued for

---

65. "How Your Mental Health Reaps the Benefits of Exercise," Sarah Gingell, PhD, *Psychology Today*, March 22, 2018, https://www.psychologytoday.com/us/blog/what-works-and-why/201803/how-your-mental-health-reaps-the-benefits-exercise.

ten to twelve weeks for the greatest antidepressant effect.[66]

R Is for Reading

Grab your self-help book and invest some time reading it—even if it's for just a few minutes. By doing this, you learn or remind yourself of an idea you can implement in your day. You might discover something new that can make you feel better, *be* better. If you're able to work up to the point that you're reading ten pages a day—ten pages, that's it—you will have read *eighteen* two-hundred-page books in a year. Can you imagine how much better your life will be and how much smarter *you'd* be if you read eighteen books a year?

Rather read fiction or something else? That has its benefits, too! No matter what you choose to read, the act of reading is exercise for your brain (and no, scrolling through the Twitter feed does not count). Reading or listening to fiction is wonderful for stress reduction, and reading anything leads to stronger focus.

It doesn't have to be a tangible book, either. Audio books work great also. I'm a big fan of Audible (https://www.audible.com/), an Amazon company. It has the world's largest selection of audiobooks and original, ad-free audio shows. I listen to Audible every morning while getting ready for work, on my commute to the office or grocery store, and while doing household chores.

---

66. "Exercise for Patients with Major Depression—What Kind of Exercise, How Intense, How Often?" Wolters Kluwer, May 10, 2013, https://wolterskluwer.com/company/newsroom/news/health/2013/05/exercise-for-patients-with-major-depression%E2%80%94what-kind-how-intense-how-often.html.

Because I read about thirty books every year, people often ask me which books I found really helpful. Here is a list of just a few of my favorites:

Book Title	Author
The 10X Rule: The Only Difference Between Success and Failure	Grant Cardone
How to Win Friends & Influence People	Dale Carnegie
The Alchemist	Paulo Coelho
Essentialism: Your Guide to the Power of Less	Mark Creed
Becoming Supernatural: How Common People Are Doing the Uncommon	Dr. Joe Dispenza
Mindset: The New Psychology of Success	Carol S. Dweck, PhD
The Miracle Morning: The Not-So-Obvious Secret Guaranteed to Transform Your Life (Before 8 AM)	Hal Elrod
Man's Search for Meaning	Dr. Viktor E. Frankl
Can't Hurt Me: Master Your Mind and Defy the Odds	David Goggins
Homo Deus: A Brief History of Tomorrow	Yuval Noah Harari
Sapiens: A Brief History of Humankind	Yuval Noah Harari
Rejection Proof: How I Beat Fear and Became Invincible Through 100 Days of Rejection	Jia Jiang
Who Moved My Cheese? An A-Mazing Way to Deal with Change in Your Work and in Your Life	Spencer Johnson
The Magic of Thinking Big	David J. Schwartz
Train Your Brain for Success: Read Smarter, Remember More, and Break Your Own Records	Roger Seip
Start with Why: How Great Leaders Inspire Everyone to Take Action	Simon Sinek

What Science Says about the Benefits of Reading

There is actually a mental health intervention based on reading. It's called *bibliotherapy*, or *reading therapy*. This treatment mainly refers to structured book-reading programs that clinics, libraries, and schools run to promote recovery in people with mental health difficulties.

Several studies have examined whether bibliotherapy can facilitate recovery from mental illness. One classic study, conducted in 1997, found a decrease in depressive symptoms after a program of bibliotherapy (therapy based on reading), a finding repeated in more recent meta-analyses and systematic reviews.[67]

More recently, in 2019, Paula Schwanenflugel, PhD, and Nancy Flanagan Knapp, PhD, the coauthors of the book *The Psychology of Reading*, noted that you don't have to read an entire book to benefit from reading. You can read short stories, picture books, and even comic books to lift your spirits![68]

In fact, the coauthors noted so many rigorous studies about the benefits of bibliotherapy that they refer to 2019 as the "year of bibliotherapy." They point to studies that were published in 2019 about the use of bibliotherapy to benefit refugee children who have suffered trauma, children with intellectual disabilities, victims of sexual abuse, adults with dementia, children with OCD, and pre-service teachers.

---

67. Nancy M. Smith, et al., "Three-Year Follow-Up of Bibliotherapy for Depression," APA PsychNET, April 1997, https://psycnet.apa.org/doiLanding?doi=10.1037%2F0022-006X.65.2.324.
68. Paula J. Schwanenflugel, PhD, and Nancy Flanagan Knapp, PhD, "Bibliotherapy: Using Books to Help and Heal," *Psychology Today*, October 1, 2019, https://www.psychologytoday.com/us/blog/reading-minds/201910/bibliotherapy-using-books-help-and-heal.

S Is for *Scribing*

Hal Elrod uses "S" for "scribing" because it works better for his acronym than "W" for "Writing." They mean the same thing. I usually use this time to jot down something I'm grateful for, a key takeaway from the reading I just did, or one of my affirmations—I switch it up depending on my mood.

Writing down our thoughts helps us retain information, and focusing on things we're grateful for puts us in an empowered, inspired, and confident state of mind.

And it helps us drown out the ugly chatter of the inner jerk.

What Science Says about the Benefits of Writing

Writing gives you a chance to be intentional about exploring your feelings, writing down positive thoughts, and expressing yourself.

Researchers at Harvard University say writing is especially beneficial following a traumatic or stressful life experience; they call this type of scribing *expressive writing*. The standard format involves writing for a specified period each day about a particularly stressful or traumatic experience.[69]

Many studies have revealed the benefits that writing

---

[69]."Writing about Emotions May Ease Stress and Trauma," Harvard Health Publishing at Harvard Medical School, https://www.health.harvard.edu/healthbeat/writing-about-emotions-may-ease-stress-and-trauma.

contributes to our physical health. It can benefit people who have physical health conditions such as sleep apnea, asthma, migraine headaches, rheumatoid arthritis, HIV, and cancer. Only recently have researchers begun to study the benefits that writing contributes to mental and emotional health.[70]

One study found that writing benefited chronically stressed caregivers of older adults. And a study by researchers at the University of Chicago found that anxious test-takers who wrote briefly about their thoughts and feelings before taking an important exam earned better grades than those who did not.

Now that you know more about the six components of a Miracle Morning, I hope you feel inspired to start following this routine tomorrow morning!

I dedicate about an hour to my Miracle Morning and save the "reading" portion for when I am getting ready to start my workday. Here's what that hour looks like:

- Silence: 10 minutes
- Affirmations: 5 minutes
- Visualization: 5 minutes
- Exercise: 30 minutes
- Reading: 30 minutes (listening to Audible while I get ready for work)
- Scribing: 10 minutes

---
70. Ibid.

If dedicating an hour doesn't seem possible, there is a shortened six-minute version; you simply do each component for one minute each. Just give it a try. The benefits are significant.

Weekly Power Hour—A Positive Way to End Each Week

The second weapon I discovered to ward off negative thoughts is my Weekly Power Hour.

While the Miracle Mornings give you focused time at the beginning of every day, the Power Hour gives you an hour to an hour and a half of additional focused time each week. I do my Power Hour on Friday afternoons for ninety minutes. That way, I can focus on the previous week and plan for the next week.

The planning you do during your Power Hour should guide your Miracle Mornings.

I grab my Panda Planner and a pen and use that time to make sure my life is organized around activities that will support my goals. That's where I do my planning to cut out all the things that don't serve me and my goals. Spending those ninety minutes helps me save myself hours of time throughout the week.

Here's what my Power Hour looks like, in six fun little steps:

1. **Reconnect with your goals.** Remember what we talked about before—begin with the end in mind. Remind yourself where you're trying to go.

2. **Review and block off your commitments.** These are the meetings or appointments you've already made plans to attend. At this point, I also ponder an intentional outcome for each of those events. For example, if it's a client meeting, what am I hoping to accomplish by the end of the meeting? Or if it's time with my family, what do I want that day to look like? For each commitment, I ask the questions, "What's my desired outcome?" and "Should that appointment/meeting/whatever even be happening at all?" One of my favorite parts of this step is actually taking things off my calendar! Before I got my shit together, I had the terrible habit of saying yes to everything.

   I have a feeling I'm not alone there! If you're in that same habit, do yourself a massive favor and learn to say no. Not only are too many commitments a recipe for stress and misery, you devalue your "yes" when you give it up to everything. (Kind of like sex.) The groundbreaking educator Peter Drucker said, "There is nothing so useless as doing efficiently that which should not be done at all." So get shit off the calendar unless it's helping you achieve your goals. The book *Essentialism* by Mark Creed helps me with this.[71] I recommend reading it.

---

71. Mark Creed, *Essentialism: Your Guide to The Power of Less: Set Your Mind with Practical Tips to Make Your Life More Manageable and Become a Happy Essentialist* (2019).

Or maybe there's a commitment that should be there, but you have allotted way more time than necessary to get it done. One thing I've learned is that your mind will use the time you allow it. If you block off forty-five minutes for an activity, your mind will use the entire forty-five minutes—even if you could have gotten it done in twenty. This concept is called Parkinson's Law.

According to Parkinson's Law, work expands to fill the time available for its completion. This concept dates back to 1955, when Cyril Northcote Parkinson, a British naval historian and author, wrote about it in *The Economist*. It's just as relevant today as ever before, though. The point is that how long something takes is largely a matter of perception.[72]

Parkinson's Law makes a similar assumption about the way people manage their money. No matter how much money people earn, they tend to spend the entire amount, plus a little bit more. Their expenses rise along with their earnings. Even though people earn much more money than they did when they began their careers, they still need every single penny to maintain their current lifestyles. No matter how much money they make, there never seems to be enough.[73]

We want to violate Parkinson's Law. We want to rise above it. We don't want to spend all the time and

---

72. Kalin Kassabov, "Four Productivity Tips for Small Business Owners," July 5, 2018, *Forbes*, https://www.forbes.com/sites/theyec/2018/07/05/four-productivity-tips-for-small-business-owners/#543ba7de7bd9.
73. "Parkinson's Law," Brian Tracy International, https://www.briantracy.com/blog/financial-success/parkinsons-law/.

money we have on frivolous things. We shouldn't give in to it. You will gain control over your time and money when you refuse to give in to Parkinson's Law.

You have to develop willpower to resist the urge to spend all your time and all your money. You have to make your best use of every second and every penny.

For example, now that I am hyper-aware of the temptation and tendency to waste time, I spend less time in meetings. I now default to shorter meetings. I used to allot one hour for team one-on-one meetings, for example, and then tried cutting them in half. What happened? We became more efficient and found that thirty minutes was plenty. We use an agenda and know exactly what we're looking to accomplish. (We have cut many of those meetings further to fifteen minutes!) Who wouldn't rather have the time back to do things other than sit in a meeting?

The same goes for household tasks. If you tell yourself you have ten minutes to clean the kitchen, you'll likely get it done in ten. If you give yourself an open window, it'll likely take twenty. Try this. It works.

3. **After reconnecting with your goals and reviewing your commitments, schedule Vitality Time and Family Time.** Vitality Time is the time spent building you as a person. It's time for *you* and nobody else. Lots of things can live in this space. For me, Vitality Time includes exercise, meditating, or getting a

massage. Don't leave this out—women, I'm talking to you. I know that we tend to get so busy taking care of everyone else—our clients, our spouses, our children, our pets—that we don't make time for ourselves. But we can't be the best version of ourselves for others if we're running on empty. We have to find time for self-care.

Look, I know how it is. Life is busy; it flies past. It often seems like there just isn't enough time to do everything that needs to get done, but what actually happens is, a sizable chunk of our time ends up getting wasted. I know, I know—you work hard to be efficient, but think about this: there are 168 hours in a week. Even if we spend 50 of those hours working, 50 of them taking care of our household, and 56 hours sleeping, that still leaves 12 whole hours a week to use however we desire. That's plenty of time for self-care, right? We just need to organize our weeks and plan to account for it.

Family Time is just what it sounds like: purposeful time to nurture the relationships closest to you. Schedule this time and guard it. Barbara Bush said, "At the end of your life, you will never regret not having passed one more test, not winning one more verdict, or not closing one more deal. You will regret time not spent with a husband, a friend, a child, a parent."

In 2013, researchers Mike Morrison and Neal Roese conducted a national survey about the regrets of a typical American. They found thirteen common sources for regret. They are, in order, related to romance, family, education, career, finance, parenting, health, "other," friends, spirituality, community, leisure, and self. The regrets overwhelmingly were about things people didn't do that they wished they had done, as opposed to doing things they wish they had not done.[74]

Relationships with your children, family, spouse, and friends are everything. Make time to grow them.

4. **Next, schedule Green Time.** *Green Time* is time that's revenue-producing. This is when you take care of things specific to work, things that are going to build your business. For a financial advisor, green time is likely going to consist of prospecting activities or client appointments. For a teacher, it's classroom time. For someone in retail, it's the time you're clocked in. For a home-based virtual assistant, it's the time you're handling tasks for your clients.

5. **After Green Time comes Red Time.** *Red Time* is all the other shit you have to get done for your work that isn't Green Time but directly supports your Green Time efforts. This includes things like getting prepared for an appointment, processing paperwork,

---

74. "Regrets of the Typical American: Findings from a Nationally Representative Sample," Mike Morrison and Neal J. Roese, Northwestern University, November 1, 2011, https://www.scholars.northwestern.edu/en/publications/regrets-of-the-typical-american-findings-from-a-nationally-repres.

commuting to your place of business, or coming up with a lesson plan.

6. **Now schedule flex time.** *Flex time* needs to be built into your calendar to allow for unexpected situations that require your attention. I call a slot for flex time on my calendar a "buffer." On my calendar, I have two buffer slots daily, each for thirty minutes.

You know how it can be. "Fires" often pop up during the day—things you didn't plan for but happen anyway and need to be addressed. The best way to make sure those fires don't detract from the other important things on your schedule is to attend to them in your flex time. Or, if it's a super-urgent fire that you to have put out on the spot, you can use your flex time to finish whatever you were working on when the "fire" started.

There needs to be a purposeful order to the way you schedule quality time. It's like getting dressed. For some items of clothing, it doesn't matter which order you put them on. But for others, it does matter. For example, it doesn't matter whether you put on your shirt or your pants first. But you *have* to put your socks on before your shoes.

Similarly, it's important to schedule Vitality Time and Family Time *before* Green Time and Red Time. If you don't make it a priority, no one else will, and you're going to run out of spots on your calendar.

What I've Accomplished as a Result of My Power Hour

As a result of my Power Hour, I have accomplished some really fun things. Here are ten of them:

1. **I made partner at my firm.** I got clear about the activities I needed to do to hit the metrics I needed to hit to make partner. If it weren't for my Power Hour, the "Got a minute?" questions and inefficiencies likely would have kept me from hitting my metrics.

2. **I lost twenty pounds.** After close to a decade of unsuccessful weight-loss efforts and yo-yo diets, I got super-serious about setting myself up for success during the week. This included finding time for a minimum of four gym workouts and planning which work meetings I could turn into walking meetings. I used to sit on my butt for ten hours straight. Now I try to have a couple of walking meetings per day. Before, I would walk 4,000 or 5,000 steps each day, and now I'm consistently at 10,000 to 15,000 steps a day. Plus, I find that my meetings feel more productive when I'm walking shoulder to shoulder next to people, versus being across from them at a boardroom table.

Small actions taken often have a big impact, too. On a daily basis, I am constantly finding ways to be healthier. For example, I take the stairs instead of the elevator. And this is going to sound crazy, but sometimes when I go to the bathroom, I'll do fifteen squats in the bathroom stall. Or if I'm on a conference call where I just have to listen, I will walk up and down my office.

3. **I completed a Spartan Race and an 80-mile bike ride.** During one of my Power Hour sessions, I made the decision to really challenge myself, and I signed up for two grueling fitness challenges. When I signed up for the bike race, I didn't even own a bike. (My beach cruiser that I hadn't ridden in seven years didn't count).

4. **I've greatly increased my mental health.** Anxiety was my normal state of being before the Power Hour. Now, with focused meditation time built in daily, time carved out for spa time once per month, and time to nurture my relationships, I have significantly less anxiety. I feel more in control of my life, which is incredibly important. When anxiety does rear its ugly head, I schedule activities to put it back in place.

5. **I've connected more with people who are important to me.** I planned time to connect with my parents and to send texts to my out-of-town best friend with a simple "Miss you and thinking of you." Before, I was running around through life, and those thoughts were an afterthought at best.

6. **I tried lots of new things:** stand-up paddleboarding, different types of workouts, different meditation techniques. I try to get at least one new thing in per month. Next, I'm going to try goat yoga.

7. **I went to a sound bath.** For centuries, healers have believed that playing or listening to instruments helps aid healing by inducing a meditative state. The practice has ancient roots in multiple cultures, including Egypt, Tibet, and Greece. Greek physicians, for example, used vibrations from flutes, lyres, and zithers to promote digestion, treat mental disturbances, and induce sleep. Much later, in Paris in the nineteenth century, a scientist named Diogel brought musicians to patients' bedsides and recorded their responses, which showed that music lowered blood pressure and pulse rate. And recent research shows that listening to the sound of water has helped reduce stress more than music or silence. The idea is to sit for a while (one to three hours, typically) in a room that is filled with the sounds of instruments like Chinese gongs, Indian shruti boxes, tuning forks, chimes, and Tibetan singing bowls.[75] I've done this, and it's incredibly relaxing and a fun experience.

8. **I wrote a book!** What you're reading now was one of my Power Hour decisions.

9. **I began having more date nights with my husband.** When we first had kids, date nights were afterthoughts. But now that I do my Power Hour regularly, it forces me to stop and think about when my husband and I can hire a sitter and go connect somewhere away from home.

---

75. Lydia Dishman, "I Tried a 'Sound Bath' to Feel Less Stressed and More Productive," *Fast Company*, May 14, 2019, https://www.fastcompany.com/90347248/i-tried-a-sound-bath-to-feel-less-stressed-and-more-productive.

10. **I've had some impactful charitable experiences.** Recently, my kids and I have been gathering up all the individual-sized toiletries like shampoo, conditioner, and lotion that we get in hotels when we travel. Then we go to the dollar store and buy toothbrushes and toothpaste. We fill bags with those items and also put a $10 bill in each one. When we see a homeless person, we give him or her one of the bags. This has been a powerful way to show our kids how they can make a difference in someone else's life. We could *tell* them how to, but this activity *shows* them how to. They get to experience for themselves how good it feels to help someone else.

I still have a long way to go to achieve balance, but these are some of the things I'm doing day-to-day to live a more positive, well-rounded life.

Sometimes we feel like if we can't make a big change, then why bother doing anything at all? But if you just start making better use of your time, a little bit here and there, those more-productive minutes will turn into more-productive hours, days, and weeks.

Maybe you have three minutes before your next meeting. What can you do to make progress toward your goals? Maybe you can scan an article, review your goals, or jot down a big idea. And try to make a little progress at a time. Trying to accomplish something huge in a short period of time can be overwhelming. If you're overwhelmed, you are less likely to reach your goal. I have found that I get more accomplished over the long term if I do a little bit at a time, and often, instead of trying to do a lot in a little bit of time.

Don't take my word for it! Implement the Power Hour into your regular routine, and you will probably be amazed at the awesome things you will accomplish. You will become more focused on what you should be doing with your time and energy, and you will become motivated once you envision yourself succeeding.

I think back to the way my life was before I had these morning and weekly routines: haphazard, chaotic, and stressful. These routines prepare me for whatever life throws at me. They keep me focused on what's really important, no matter who (I'm talkin' to you, Lucy) or what tries to derail my plans and my happy mood.

CHAPTER 6

Connections

"When you hang out with whiners, pessimists, tweakers, bleakers, freakers-outers, and life-is-so-unfairers, it's an uphill climb to keep yourself in a positive headspace. Stay away from people with tiny minds and tiny thoughts, and start hanging out with people who see limitless possibility as the reality. Surround yourself with people who act on their big ideas, who take action on making positive change in the world, and who see nothing as out of their reach."

—Jen Sincero, Author of
You Are a Badass

People matter. Who you surround yourself with matters.

When we surround ourselves with positive people, we are more likely to be positive, too.

Since the beginning of time, humans have needed one another. The earliest populations formed tribes to share responsibilities related to hunting, cooking, caring for children, and watching out for predators. Just because our lives are filled with technology now doesn't mean that has changed. But today, we call our tribes "teams."

When you are building a team, you want to surround yourself with people who excel in different areas and people who lift you up rather than bring you down. This is just as true at home as it is in the office. (Lucy didn't make the roster.)

Let's start by talking about business.

Build a Strong Team

We cannot excel in organizations by working alone. Stephen Covey's concept of *interdependence* is based on the fact that when everyone pools their unique talents in a team effort, the overall result is much more profound than if each team member had acted alone.

This rings so true for me. During my professional journey, naysayers have told me I didn't have the skill set to be a Managing Director. They were actually right. By myself, I don't have all the skills. I am actually really bad at a lot of the skills it takes to run a successful practice and office.

But I do have the confidence to admit my handicaps, and I have the intelligence to build a team around me that is great where I am not. That's how I have been able to build the incredible office I have today. To build a great organization—whatever industry you're in—you need different personalities and skills on your team. You need visionaries, integrators, marketing gurus, recruiting masters, detail people, big-picture people, IT experts…you get the idea.

Don't try to be all things to all people. Pick a swim lane, and focus on *your* highest and best use. Build a team to support the rest. Take a real look at the things you love to do, the things that energize you, and the things you want to do all day long. Then make a list of all the other things—the things you don't love and that you're not good at. Build a team to do all the things you don't want to do so you can stay in your own swim lane and focus on what you are amazing at.

Sometimes, leaders and really competitive people hesitate to give up some of their responsibilities. They want to believe they excel at everything. I believe that, as leaders, we need to check our egos at the door. There is always going to be someone better, someone faster, and someone smarter at certain aspects of any business. Find those people. Partner with them. Make them the force on *your* side of the table.

I strongly believe that dynamic teaming is the wave of the future for all businesses. Whatever type of business you're in, people expect and deserve experts, and no matter how amazing you are, you can't be an expert in everything.

So partner with other people who possess the skills you don't have.

Women, Listen Up!

When I talk about building a team, I'm not just talking about work. We need to build a team on the domestic front as well.

As women, we tend to try to do everything ourselves. We don't ask for help. We run our businesses, we run our kids' schedules, we do all the holiday planning, we cook all the meals, we clean the house, and we do the laundry. It's like we think we get a special badge if we do it all. Well, I'm here to tell you, there's no badge! Get some damn help!

A good first step is to hire a house cleaner. I used to have an absolute aversion to hiring a house cleaner. It's probably because I grew up hearing someone call people "lazy" if they didn't clean their own houses. (Lucy says the same thing.) So subconsciously, I couldn't get myself to delegate that time-consuming job to someone else.

But I would rather spend time playing with my kids than cleaning my toilets. So I have a house cleaner now, and I have a lot of clothing dry-cleaned to cut back on laundry. I also use a grocery-delivery service several times a month. And best of all, I just hired a mother's helper. She comes to my house two nights a week for three hours and helps me with the boys' lunches and does laundry.

It has been fabulous, but some people have made negative comments to me, jabbing at me a little bit, like, "Oh, it must be nice to be able to afford that" or "It must be nice to not have to do those things on your own." At first, I struggled with that. But then I realized those comments aren't about me; they're about other people.

We all make choices about how we spend our money. How I choose to spend mine is a personal decision, and that's the topic of the next chapter.

You deserve help, and it's OK to ask for it! Whatever type of help you need, arrange for it. Create your own tribe. What does that look like for you? Maybe it's having GrubHub or DoorDash deliver your dinner. Maybe it's having an Uber driver pick up your out-of-town visitors from the airport. Maybe it's hiring someone to mow your lawn.

You don't have to spend money to get some help, though. You can share responsibilities with your friends and neighbors. People in Sweden live by this principle. It's called *Jantelagen*, or the Law of Jante. This informal law suggests that no one is better than anyone, from the CEO to the janitor—everyone is equal. The Law of Jante is reflected in the societal behavior of Scandinavian countries: Finland, Sweden, Norway, Denmark, and Iceland. This popular social code emphasizes collective achievement and well-being, and it shuns the focus on individual achievements.

An article from the *International Policy Digest* says the Western mindset of winning, no matter what, has proven to be ineffective in bringing happiness. In March 2019, on the International Day of Happiness, the Happiness Research Institute released its latest World Happiness Report. The report focuses on happiness and the community. As usual, Scandinavian countries rank among the ten happiest countries. In spite of its economic success, the United States ranks nineteenth. The article concludes by saying, "In sum, everyone could benefit from a more communal society such as the Swedish. Everyone says they want the world to be a better place—belonging to a trusting, supportive community may be the solution to that. Adapting and integrating a collective mindset and the Law of Jante would increase a sense of cooperation and collectivism, and therefore, contribute to more happiness."[76]

Amen to that!

If money is tight and hiring help isn't an option, find other people in your community who want to trade and share responsibilities. Let's say you have five neighbors. Neighbor 1 could make dinner on Monday night for all five households. Neighbor 2 takes Tuesday, and so on. Then, instead of all five households having to worry about dinner every night, each person has to make dinner only one night per week. You can do the same thing with child care. One mom can watch all the kids on Monday evening, and another mom can watch them on Tuesday, and so on. This frees up massive amounts of time, and it builds a strong community.

So go make friends with those neighbors you've never met!

We need to support each other as we all strive to reach

---

76. Patricia Zanini Graca, "The Swedish Model of Success and Happiness," *International Policy Digest*, June 4, 2019, https://intpolicydigest.org/2019/06/04/the-swedish-model-of-success-and-happiness/.

our vision. Don't try to do everything alone. And don't let some asshole try to make you feel guilty for asking for help.

Separate Yourself from Negative People

When we're putting our tribes together, we need to make sure everyone we choose to spend time with has a positive influence on us. One reason we tend to wallow in negativity and let negative thoughts take over is that some of the people we spend time with are negative. They are toxic influences in our lives, and we must separate ourselves from them.

I knew people in my life for over a decade, and they were some of my closest friends. But as I grew up, I realized that we no longer had the same interests, and our values weren't aligned anymore. Being friends with them no longer fit into my vision of where I wanted to go in the future. So over the years, I have separated myself from them. It was tough, sad, and sometimes contentious. But mostly, we just drifted apart.

Maybe you have known someone since kindergarten. As you've grown up, it's likely that your values have changed. When you were playing in the sandbox together, you shared interests. But things are different now. Don't be afraid to be choosy about the people you spend time with. It's a necessary step in your growth.

Motivational speaker Jim Rohn said we are the average of the five people we spend the most time with. If you're spending time with toxic people, that isn't healthy for you. Make the changes that are necessary to spend time only with people who are positive, optimistic, and encouraging.

These choices are important in both your personal life and business.

Coaches deal with this every day. Even top-performing players are sometimes cut from the team if they don't follow the rules or fit the team culture anymore.

Professional athletes tend to have big egos. There are plenty of stories out there about talented athletes who are booted from their team rosters for serious violations, such as domestic violence or doping. Other infractions are less serious but still show a lack of character, a lack of team spirit, or a lack of respect for their coach and teammates.

In my firm, we have parted ways with quite a few team members who weren't aligned with our values and culture. In some cases, those team members were top performers, so it was a bold move for us to terminate them and lose the revenue they brought in. But we have never regretted any of those decisions.

On the flip side, there have been many times we have regretted letting the wrong person linger for too long.

So how do you know when it's time for someone to go? If I cringe when I see someone's name pop up on my caller ID, that's a good indication that he or she isn't a great fit with our firm, or I shouldn't be friends with that person. If I had a party at my house, would I invite that person because I wanted to or because I felt obligated to? Also, if the people around you seem to agree that a certain person is eroding trust, taking advantage of people, or treating customers or team members badly, it's time to cut them loose.

If someone on your team, whether in your personal life or at work, is pulling you and everyone else down, it might be time to cut him or her from your roster.

I believe that you're either in or you're in the way. Figure out who is in. Who wants to be on your team, on your side? Stop wasting your energy on those who are in your way.

Get a Mentor

One of the most powerful connections you'll ever have is a mentor.

I've mentioned many examples of a coach helping me in one aspect or another. I'm a huge fan of mentorship and coaching. Mentors have played a role in my life for as long as I can remember.

Bill, my first Taekwondo instructor, and his instructor, Master Aleem, were great influences. In high school, my mentor was Mr. Thelen, the theater teacher.

In college, mentors came in unlikely areas. Sean, a multimillionaire business owner, was a regular at the restaurant where I bartended. He would spend his meal breaks giving me advice on how to be successful in business and in life. One time, he let me drive his Phantom Rolls Royce for one lap around the parking lot! I knew I wanted to be successful like Sean one day, so I hung onto every piece of advice he gave. I don't know if he even realized he was mentoring me. He probably just thought we were just having great conversations.

In business, I have been fortunate enough to have many amazing mentors throughout the years. They have taken me under their wings and given me incredible opportunities. They help talk me off the ledge when times are tough and give me a boost when I have not been quite tall enough to reach my goal.

In addition to mentors, I've had a professional coach for the past decade of my career. Coaches are different than mentors in that coaching relationships are typically, but not always, short-term relationships focused on performance-driven goals. Coaches are professionals I pay to help me reach peak performance for whatever goal I have in mind. I started hiring coaches before I felt financially ready to, and guess what? It was totally worth it. They stretched me to grow, and I always made that money back, sometimes tenfold.

The best of the best all have coaches—the best athletes, the best musicians, the best businesspeople—someone to critique them and help them get even better. Whether you're a businessperson, a teacher, or a stay-at-home parent, get a mentor and coach to help you get better. Seek out people whom you aspire to be like, and ask for their help.

Hire a coach before you think you can afford to. Doing so will pay for itself.

Tips for Connecting

For some people, connecting with others comes naturally. Other people struggle with it. Since this chapter is all about connection, here are some tips for making valuable connections in your life:

1. **Don't be an asshole.** I know this statement seems like *duh*, but I don't think this is as obvious as it should be because I know a lot of assholes. The word "frenemy"—a combination of "friend" and "enemy"—is way too mainstream these days. That's because even some of the people who are your friends act like assholes. Don't be one of them!

2. **Be thoughtful.** This one is a continual work in progress for me. With two kids, two businesses (I help my husband with his business) and other day-to-day responsibilities, it takes extra effort for me to be thoughtful. I've got it pretty mastered in my business, but I'm still working on this in my personal relationships. Here are some things I do for the people in my business:

    A. **We give everyone a welcome package when they join our team.** It's a small effort to make someone feel super-happy they joined us.

    B. **We mail written birthday cards to our team members' businesses.** Today, in a world where everyone sends you a birthday message on Facebook, including your own mom, a handwritten birthday card goes a long way. It's unexpected and appreciated.

    C. **We celebrate milestones.** At the one-year anniversary of someone joining our team, we send a card and a company-branded blanket to the team member and his or her spouse, letting them know how grateful we are to have them as a part of the family. We also celebrate other milestone anniversaries and life events.

In my personal life, I want to make it a point to ping three people a week just to check in and say hello. I also typically end up hosting the barbecues or pool parties for our group of friends.

3. **Be better about remembering names.** In *How to Win Friends and Influence People*, self-improvement guru Dale Carnegie says, "Remember that a person's name is to that person the sweetest and most important sound in any language." Remembering names of customers, prospects, team members, networking contacts, and colleagues is critical to your ongoing professional success. I keep a list in my phone of the names of people, their spouses, their children, and their pets. In today's age of technology and tools at your fingertips, there's just no excuse not to remember someone's name. It definitely solidifies the relationship when I can say, "Hey, Bonnie, how is Mike?" even though I met Mike only once. That extra effort to care about the things and relationships that are important to people is critical.

Some people may think that storing names in my phone is inauthentic. I see it as making an extra effort. I'm just using technology to help me with my authentic interest in their lives.

4. **Be kind.** This kind of goes along with not being an asshole, but I want to elaborate a little bit. Everyone is doing the best they can with what they know. I realize this now, but I used to be super-judgmental. If I felt like someone wasn't as "enlightened" as I was, I couldn't believe it. After all, we all have access to the same information on the internet; there's no excuse for ignorance. But then, as I started learning more about the subconscious brain and how our experiences from our past shape our current lens, it taught me to be a kinder, less judgmental person. It made me realize we are all humans trying to navigate life the best we know how. I became less quick to get frustrated with the fast-food worker who screwed up my order or the person who made ignorant comments on Facebook. It taught me to pray for wisdom for that person and send positive vibes their way, instead of being passive-aggressive or rude to them. If everyone were a little more intentional about radiating love and kindness, this world would be a much better place.

5. **Segment your relationships.** "This is common in the business world. We differentiate our A-plus clients from our A, B, and C clients, based on revenue, referrals, or some other metric, and we define the parameters for each tier. I think it makes sense to do the same in your personal life, too. It's hard to go deep with those who matter most to you if you're spread too thin, trying to please everybody. Give those who are the most precious to you priority in your schedule. Don't miss your best friend's birthday

party because you committed to a birthday party for a six-year-old neighbor whose mom you've talked to only twice. Too often, I see people struggle with prioritizing their relationships. This goes back to what we talked about earlier: learn to say no, and know that it's OK to take things off your calendar.

6. **Laugh a lot.** People want to connect with other happy people. I think many of us take life too seriously. Humans are energy, and you can tell what kind of energy people carry the moment they walk into a room. If you are that person who walks around like Eeyore, the gloomy donkey from *Winnie the Pooh*, it's going to be hard to connect. Maybe my energy is too much for some people at times, but I'll take Tigger over Eeyore any day of the week. (You might remember that laughter is one of my values. It's super-important to me.)

Maybe you've never thought about the way you connect with people. Make it a priority to be intentional about surrounding yourself with positive people.

How are you showing up? One exercise I've used multiple times in business is to ask people in both my personal and business life to describe and assess me in key areas. The answers are anonymous, so you don't know who said what—but you get honest feedback. It's tough to hear the truth sometimes, but you will never get better if you don't know how you're showing up.

Check in with your spouse, your friends, and your colleagues. Ask them how you can better contribute to the relationship.

Divorce is on a down trend, but it's still high. Maybe divorce would be less common if people did a better job of nurturing their relationships and checking in with each other before they are upset with each other, before it's too late.

When people first start dating, they put in a ton of time and effort trying to wow each other and win them over. Then, when they finally commit to each other, it seems like that effort just stops. We try so hard in the beginning of a relationship! Once the slightest disagreement comes up, we don't try to work it out. No wonder divorce is so common.

I think this is true of many relationships, not just with a spouse or partner. I encourage you to really reflect on how you are nurturing your most important relationships. Are you putting in the effort to really make them thrive?

CHAPTER 7
Your Financial House

"Do not save what is left after spending, but spend what is left after saving."

—Warren Buffett

Now we're going to switch gears a little and talk about finances. Money issues have a huge impact on our self-worth and on our relationships. I want to provide some suggestions for optimizing your finances. When you do, you will gain leverage in every area of your life.

You can't focus on your vision, remain positive, and be on the top of your game if you are always worried about money. Because I have built my career in financial services, I witness every day the role that financial health plays in people's happiness and quality of life.

So, although this isn't intended to be a book about financial management, I do want to share some basic concepts about getting your financial house in order. If your inner jerk is telling you it's OK to drop $1,000 on a few things at Amazon because you've had a rough day, you need to muster your courage, conviction, and confidence to send that inner jerk packing.

Businesses fail, households fail, and relationships fail when finances are not in good order.

The basics of financial health include living within your means; getting organized; knowing exactly where your money is; protecting your number-one asset—your income; and making sure you have enough money to live well, no matter what happens. Let's look at each of these steps in detail.

Six Steps to Getting Control of Your Finances

Although getting your financial house in order isn't the focus of this book, this topic is incredibly important in maintaining control over your finances and planning well for the future. I will take you through an abbreviated version of the six-step process we take our clients through.

1. Get Organized

Earlier, I recommended inspecting your schedule to find out where you are spending your time. It's important to do the same type of exercise with your finances so you know where your money is going. Review at least one quarter's worth of expenses, and document where every dime goes. Our clients are often shocked to see where they're spending their money. Sometimes, they cannot even account for where the money went. For example, they withdraw $500 from the ATM and have no idea what they spent it on. Inspecting where your cash is going is a critical first step in gaining control of your finances.

Another critical component of this stage is thinking through your goals and concerns. We talked a lot about vision and goals earlier in the book. How do your goals apply to finances? What things are most important to you? Is it important that you save enough to provide a debt-free college education to your children? Do you want to save enough for a down payment on your first home? Is making sure that you have enough saved for the retirement of your dreams front of mind? Organizing your thoughts around these priorities will help you take the necessary steps toward achieving your financial goals.

2. Protect Your Income

Your number-one asset is your ability to generate an income. It's not your 401(k) account or your house—it's *you*.

A twenty-five-year-old who is making $50,000 per year and getting small 3 percent raises regularly means her income is worth $3,7000,000 over her entire career. For someone who earns $100,000 per year, that lifetime income jumps to $7,500,000.

I remember so vividly the moment I grasped this. It was during one of my college finance classes, and we had a guest speaker come in who was a financial advisor. He asked the class this question: "If you had a machine in your garage that would spit out millions of dollars of cash to you over your lifetime, would you insure it?"

The entire class responded with a resounding, "Yes, of course." There was even a "Duh!" response.

He then went on to reveal that the machine in the garage he was talking about was us, as humans, He showed an illustration similar to the numbers I just shared about our income potential over the course of our careers. Next, he asked us if we had ever heard of income protection or disability insurance, and the room got quiet—none of us had. He wrapped up the session by explaining products available to protect our income: disability insurance, life insurance, and a few others.

I was a senior, about to graduate with a finance degree, and in theory, my curriculum was teaching me all the ways to help people with their finances upon graduation. I had learned all about how to analyze risk/reward in the stock market. Terms like *beta*, *alpha*, and *Sharpe Ratio* were common calculations I was tested on. I learned about bonds and interest rate sensitivity and coupon rates. I learned about real estate, mortgage loans, banking concepts, etc. But not *once* had anyone in my classes talked about protecting a machine that would spit out millions of dollars.

I share this story with you because, even as someone who was groomed to focus on finance, I was in the dark about how important protection is.

You must put protection strategies in place to protect your future income. Various insurance products will protect your income against a lawsuit, death, or becoming sick or injured. Unfortunately, most of the American public is either completely unprotected or grossly underinsured. Many times, it's because of a lack of awareness around protection products or an assumption that these products are too "expensive." Sometimes though, it's a priority issue.

It saddens me when I speak to people with children who will spend $30 per month protecting their precious iPhones (which cost them $1,100), but they say they don't have the money to buy life insurance. For $30 per month, most healthy people can qualify for term insurance to help protect their families' financial future.

I see these same people spending hundreds of dollars a month eating out, but they opt out of purchasing disability insurance that will help protect their income, should they become sick or injured. They think it will never happen to them. But the reality is that more than one in four of today's twenty-year-olds can expect to be out of work for at least a year because of a disabling condition before they reach age sixty-seven (the normal retirement age). Nearly 6 percent of working Americans will experience a short-term disability (six months or less) due to illness, injury, or pregnancy, on average, *every year*.[77]

Please don't make the mistake of thinking that worker's compensation or Social Security Disability Income (SSDI) will cover these costs. Take a look at these statistics:

- Workers' compensation covers only time away from work if the disabling illness or injury was directly work-related. In 2016, only 1 percent of American workers missed work because of an occupational illness or injury.[78]

- From 2006 to 2015, only 34 percent of SSDI claimants had their applications approved—23 percent at the initial application stage and the remainder after a reconsideration or appeals process.[79]

- It generally takes three to five months from time of application for SSDI benefits to get an initial decision. The backlog of appeals cases was

---

77. "The Crisis of Disability Coverage in America," Council for Disability Awareness, http://disabilitycanhappen.org/public_html/wp-content/uploads/2018/04/The-CDA-RealityCheckup-Media-Kit.pdf.
78. Ibid.
79. Ibid.

more than one million in 2017, with associated processing time averaging more than 18 months.[80]

- The average SSDI benefit as of January 2018 was $1,197 a month. That equates to $14,364 annually—barely above the poverty guideline of $12,140 for a one-person household, and below the guideline of $16,640 for a two-person household.[81]

Please don't view this discussion as fearmongering. We don't want to assume the worst can happen. But we also can't ignore the statistics, and we need to be prepared in case the worst does in fact happen.

Protect your income. Protect your family. Take responsibility. Ever notice how many GoFundMe pages pop up on Facebook these days? And those cans in local restaurants, asking for donations to help pay for the funeral of someone who died without life insurance? Don't let this happen to your family!

At our firm, we teach our clients the 3 F's of protection:

- Protect first.
- Protect fully.
- Protect for as long as the risk is present.

There are many complexities to protection products. I highly recommend that you work with a licensed professional rather than to try to go it alone.

---
80. Ibid.
81. Ibid.

3. Live Within Your Means

Living within your means requires that you build up world-class savings through a detailed understanding of cash flow. In our materialistic society, we're often encouraged to "fake it till we make it." People buy expensive houses, cars, and boats so people will think they're doing well.

It's my firm belief that we need to stop doing this. I have personally seen people make millions of dollars who were completely broke because they spent so much trying to keep up with an image. They lived beyond their means.

At our firm, we teach our clients to become world-class savers and save a minimum of 15 to 20 percent of their gross income annually. That's great advice for anyone of any age, in any walk of life.

I encourage you to look at your own finances and ask yourself if you are living within your means and saving enough for the future. If not, some changes are in order. This might mean downsizing your home or getting a roommate. Maybe you need to forget about upgrading to the newest iPhone just because your lease is paid off on the older version and you're eligible for an upgrade.

I mentioned earlier that our income is our greatest asset. Being efficient with how we spend that cash flow is the greatest resource we have to achieve our financial goals and build long-term wealth.

But don't worry, it's not all about cutting down on your beloved Starbucks runs. Efficiency in cash flow includes making sure you are not overpaying in taxes because you are not up to speed with the latest tax mitigation strategies, that you are not overpaying for your debt obligations, that you are not overpaying for various types of insurance, and the like. Work with a financial professional who can help you look at all these areas. He or she can help you achieve your goals for the future and also have money left over to enjoy your current life.

4. Establish a Life-Event Fund/Liquidity Reserves

Life happens. The transmission on your car breaks, the air conditioner in your house suddenly stops working in the dead heat of summer, or your kid breaks an arm sliding into home plate, incurring a medical bill you weren't prepared for.

Even if these types of events aren't catastrophic, they can have catastrophic effects on your future finances if you are not prepared for them. Putting a $2,000 medical bill on a credit card at a 19 percent interest rate can snowball your debt to an unmanageable level if you pay only the minimum payment.

On the other hand, having liquidity in a life-event fund prevents you from ever needing to put those expenses on a credit card, and it allows you to stay focused on your long-term wealth building. A good first step is to save up $1,000 into a liquidity account. That would help if one or two small events came about. But don't stop there. A minimum of three to six months of expenses built up in a life-event fund is necessary. We encourage our clients to keep building that fund until they save a full year of income.

5. Eliminate Short-Term Debt

Not all debt is bad. Some debt can be useful in a long-term wealth-accumulation strategy. Debt for a mortgage on a home or a business line of credit to expand your business can be a good leveraging tactic. But short-term, high-interest rate debt is a killer to any financial plan. It's like trying to run a marathon with a 50-lb. shackle tied to your ankle. Having that burden, it will take you much longer to get to the finish line—if you ever get there at all.

Short-term debt includes car notes, credit cards, and student loans. Eliminating that debt as quickly and efficiently as possible—and continuing to stay out of debt—is crucial to achieving your financial goals.

There are several different methods to paying down debt. I will share a couple of methods using the following example.

Let's assume someone has debt as follows:

Type of Debt	Amount of Debt	Interest Rate
Credit Card A	$8,000	19%
Credit Card B	$5,000	11%
Credit Card C	$1,000	15%
Car Note	$17,000	6%

A. Snowball Method

With the snowball method, you pay off your lowest account balance first. Once that account is paid off, you proceed to the next-larger debt, and so forth, proceeding to the largest debt last. Using the accounts above, the snowball method would pay off Credit Card C first while making minimum payments on all other accounts. Once Credit Card C is paid off, Credit Card B would be tackled next, followed by Credit Card A, followed by the car note. Here are the debts in that order:

Type of Debt	Amount of Debt	Interest Rate
Credit Card C	$1,000	15%
Credit Card B	$5,000	11%
Credit Card A	$8,000	19%
Car Note	$17,000	6%

Mathematically, the snowball method isn't always the best, though. Sometimes, it causes you to pay lower-interest-rate debt off prior to higher-interest-rate debt. In the example above, you paid off Credit Card B, which had an 11 percent interest rate, while accruing higher interest of 19 percent on Credit Card A.

However, the entire focus of this book has been the mind and its power. Psychologically, sometimes we need a "win" to gather the willpower to continue our strategy. And the "win" of paying off an account completely and having no more balance on it can sometimes make the snowball strategy worthwhile.

B. Avalanche Method

With the avalanche method, you pay your debts from the highest interest rate to the lowest interest rate, regardless of the balances on the accounts. Using our example above, you would put all efforts into paying off Credit Card A while paying the minimum payments on every other account. Once Card A is paid off, you would pay off Card C, followed by Card B, and finally your car note.

Mathematically, this makes the most sense. You will pay less in interest if you pay your debts in this order. Saving on interest, in turn, helps you pay off your debts more quickly. Here is what the avalanche method looks like in our example:

Type of Debt	Amount of Debt	Interest Rate
Credit Card A	$8,000	19%
Credit Card C	$1,000	15%
Credit Card B	$5,000	11%
Car Note	$17,000	6%

There are other strategies for debt reduction, but they are beyond the scope of this book. Regardless of which debt-reduction strategy you choose, getting out of debt—and staying out of short-term debt—is critical. The mental freedom you will feel once you are free from short-term debt is incredible, and it will help you focus your efforts on long-term wealth accumulation.

6. Create Long-Term Wealth Accumulation

This is the fun and sexy part of your financial planning, and it's where we see most clients wanting to focus their time and attention. This phase involves building your retirement accounts, college education accounts for your children, or savings for other goals. The psychological reward of seeing these accounts grow and getting closer to realizing your dreams is amazing.

We talked about reconnecting with your vision at least once per week in earlier chapters. I encourage you to do the same with your financial goals so it is easier to stick to your budget. It's a lot easier to pass up that sale when you remind yourself of the rewards your financial discipline will lead to.

Here's a tip: nickname your accounts if your financial institution allows for it. For example, rather than having your child's 529 account be listed as ABC100002, call it "Jackson's debt-free college education." When you see the goal associated with the account rather than the digits the institution assigns to it, you are more likely to contribute to the account.

Dr. Daniel Crosby is a psychologist, behavioral finance expert, and bestselling author on the topic of market psychology. According to his research, earmarking an account with the goal behind it (i.e., having your children's names associated with the nickname on an account) nearly doubles the savings rate to the account. As your savings buckets become less abstract and more personally meaningful, you are more likely to change or improve your behavior. It's a small psychological trick with amazing results!

The way you handle your finances is directly related to how likely you are to achieve your vision. Every time you make a decision about money, you are affecting your future and your family's future. Don't let those negative voices in your mind—that bitch, that inner jerk—tell you it's OK to blow your budget just to feel better, or to compete with someone by buying expensive things you don't need.

Remember what's really important. Make every financial decision with your vision in clear focus.

A curious mind is a healthy mind. In my presentations, I often refer to the quote from Ray Kroc. I say, "You're either green and growing or ripe and dying. Which are *you*?"

People who are green and growing are always learning, up until they take their last breaths. People who don't read or listen to other people's wisdom are ripe and dying. It's interesting to see what happens when people reach their eighties. Some of them are sitting in their houses, waiting to die. Others are out there in the world, still contributing their own wisdom and still learning everything they can.

In 2019, Bob Dwyer, age ninety, became Northeastern Illinois University's oldest graduate since records were first kept in 1962. In a TV interview, Dwyer said, "It's never going to be too late, and I think the reward is worth it. I am curious by nature." After he served in the US Army, got married, and had a successful career, he decided to go back to school.[82]

Bob Dwyer is green and growing.

It would have been easy for this gentleman to say, "Oh, well, I missed my chance to finish my education." But he didn't. He said, "I'm going to finish my education!" And he did. What an inspiration!

In fact, being an active learner can actually slow down cognitive decline.

---

82. "Never Too Late: 90-Year-Old Graduates College 70 Years After Dropping Out to Join US Army," Action News 6, WPVI-TV Philadelphia, May 8, 2019, https://www.wtae.com/article/100-year-old-man-gets-degree-from-duquesne-university/8509240.

Researchers have discovered many benefits of lifelong learning:[83]

- A *Harvard Business Review* article noted that reading, even for short periods of time, can dramatically reduce your stress levels.

- A recent report in *Neurology* noted that while cognitive activity can't change the biology of Alzheimer's, learning activities can help delay symptoms, preserving people's quality of life.

- Research shows that learning to play a new musical instrument can offset cognitive decline, and learning difficult new skills in older age is associated with improved memory.

- And 2006 research suggests that a year of formal education can add more than half a year to a person's life span.

What classes have you always wanted to take that you didn't have time for in college? What is a topic that has always interested you, but you never took the time to really dive into? Imagine the conversation-starters you'll have at cocktail parties when you take a class on an interesting topic at your local junior college, community center, or other location. Or maybe you've always wanted to learn a new language. Go for it!

---

83. John Coleman, :Lifelong Learning Is Good for Your Health, Your Wallet, and Your Social Life," *Harvard Business Review*, February 2, 2017, https://hbr.org/2017/02/lifelong-learning-is-good-for-your-health-your-wallet-and-your-social-life.

We should never stop learning. I go to probably ten conferences per year for business. I also go to at least one conference to learn about personal growth and development. For personal development, I have taken courses in nutrition, longevity, mind–body connection, language, and art. Some of these learning opportunities are in person, and some are virtual. I love to travel, so one of my favorite things to do is scope out destination learning opportunities. I most recently went to Sedona, Arizona, to see Dr. Joe Dispenza. Sedona is magical, and Dr. Joe is amazing. Before I had the income to afford travel to amazing places like Sedona, I took advantage of free online learning.

I would pick topics I wanted to learn more about and research those topics online, borrow books from friends about them, or go to the library (yes, there are people who still go to a physical library—well, at least before the pandemic).

Did you know that you can take 140 classes from Harvard completely free?! Harvard University, where tuition exceeds $45K per year, will allow you to take its courses at absolutely no expense. Harvard isn't the only Ivy League university providing free courses. You can take courses from Brown, Cornell, Princeton, Yale...the list goes on and on.

I also love using applications for learning. Right now I am working on basic Spanish through an app called Duolingo. The app is completely free and has fun games to help you learn different languages. It features more than thirty-five languages (Latin, Swahili, and Hawaiian, to name a few).

Build learning into your vision, your goals, and your values. Build it into your life. Read more, listen to podcasts, attend seminars, travel...just be committed to making use of the phenomenal brain you are equipped with. When you learn more, you will feel more confident. And that confidence is a powerful weapon against Lucy and her gang.

Phew! We made it to the end. Many times throughout this writing process, Lucy told me I would never get to this point and I wouldn't accomplish publishing this book. Well, she can f-off because...here it is! My hope when writing this book was to share my personal journey and the tangible, tactical actions that have worked for me. I hope you have gleaned at least one idea that will make you feel your time spent reading it was worth it. (After all, I preached about how precious time is, so I don't want to be a contributor to wasting yours!)

I've made a lot of suggestions in this book, but I absolutely don't want it to come across like I have all this shit figured out. I don't. I have worked really hard over the years, and I've made progress, but I still have to box that bitch pretty often. I've read plenty of articles and books by people who pretend like they've figured it *all* out. Hold onto your seat because I am going to share a crazy secret: they haven't! I think it's important that we stop pretending to be perfect and embrace the journey of continual improvement. None of us has this crazy thing called life totally figured out. We are perfectly imperfect, and all we can do is work daily to continue to get better.

I'm not sure any of us ever get to stop boxing those bitches who try to keep us from succeeding, but we can certainly get to the point where it's easier.

We have to *choose* to focus on the positive. When we are bombarded from all directions with gloom and doom, we cannot get caught up in it. We must be aware of what we're allowing to influence our thoughts. We must be the gatekeepers of our own minds. We must leverage positivity, science, and personal choices to make our minds work for us, not against us.

About the Author

Misty Weltzien, CLU®, ChFC®, CFP®
misty_weltzien@pacificadvisors.com
pacificadvisors.com/misty_weltzien

Misty Weltzien is a mom, wife, daughter, friend, and business owner striving daily to make herself less of a self-proclaimed "disaster." She believes in the continual pursuit of self-improvement and striving to make the world a better place. She is an advocate for women in her profession, adores people and animals, and is a travel junkie.

In her journey of personal development, Misty has learned many things along the way that helped guide her. She is excited to share those lessons with anyone who will listen. Her hobbies include spa days, wine tasting, and belting out "Bust a Move" at karaoke bars.

This material has not been endorsed by Guardian, its subsidiaries, agents, or employees. No representation or warranty, either express or implied, is provided in relation to the accuracy, completeness, or reliability of the information contained herein. In addition, the content does not necessarily represent the opinions of Guardian, its subsidiaries, agents, or employees. Material discussed is meant for general informational purposes only and is not to be construed as tax, legal, or investment advice. Please note that individual situations can vary. Therefore, the information should be relied upon only when coordinated with individual professional advice. Links and information regarding external sites or services are provided for your convenience in locating related information and services. Guardian, its subsidiaries, agents, and employees expressly disclaim any responsibility for and do not maintain, control, recommend, or endorse third-party sites, organizations, products, or services and make no representation as to the completeness, suitability, or quality thereof.

Misty Weltzien is a Registered Representative and Financial Advisor of Park Avenue Securities LLC (PAS). OSJ: 333 N Indian Hill Blvd, Claremont, CA 91711, 909-399-1100. Securities products and advisory services offered through PAS, member FINRA, SIPC. General Agent of The Guardian Life Insurance Company of America® (Guardian), New York, NY. PAS is a wholly owned subsidiary of Guardian. Pacific Advisors LLC is not an affiliate or subsidiary of PAS or Guardian. AR insurance license #10319821, CA insurance license #0F97449. 2020-113796. Exp. 12/22.

www.ingramcontent.com/pod-product-compliance
Lightning Source LLC
Chambersburg PA
CBHW060836220526
45466CB00003B/1130